GOOD [GEN]ERAL FURNISHINGS. DRUGS. GROCERIES LIV[E]

CALIFORNIA

I GOT IT
AT
H. E. GARD'S
INDIO CAL

H. E. GARD
GENERAL
MERCHANDISE

Coachella Valley California

A Pictorial History

is made possible by the generous support of

Golden Acre Farms

Valley Independent Bank

John F. Kennedy Memorial Hospital

Clark's UltraMar Auto-Truck Stop and Store

Anita Carter Ellis

Paul Ames

Ray and Marlene House

Proceeds from the sale of this volume will be used to benefit programs
of the Coachella Valley Museum and Historical Society

Coachella Valley California

A Pictorial History

by Patricia B. Laflin

Patricia B. Laflin
December 1998

THE
DONNING COMPANY
PUBLISHERS

The Donning Company/Publishers
184 Business Park Drive, Suite 106
Virginia Beach, VA 23462

Steve Mull, General Manager
Barbara A. Bolton, Project Director
Dawn V. Kofroth, Assistant General Manager
Shannon H. Garza, Associate Editor
Percival J. Tesoro, Graphic Designer
Teri S. Arnold, Senior Marketing Coordinator

Library of Congress Cataloging-in-Publication Data:

Laflin, Patricia B., 1927–
    Coachella Valley, California : a pictorial history / by Patricia
B. Laflin
        p.   cm.
    Includes index.
    ISBN 1-57864-049-0 (alk. paper)
    1. Coachella Valley (Calif.)—History. 2. Coachella Valley
(Calif.)—History—Pictorial works. I. Title.
F868.R6L34 1998
979.4'97—dc21   98-33803
                                                                    CIP

Printed in the United States of America

Contents

Introduction

Driving east from Los Angeles on Interstate 10, there is a view from the summit of Whitewater Grade which is breathtaking beyond any description of it. To the southeast, stretches the Coachella Valley—the northern end of the great Imperial Valley. One of the world's largest sand dunes, seventeen miles in length, meanders down the center of this portion of the Colorado Desert. The dune is the locale of the Annenberg Estate, Mission Hills Country Club, and portions of Cathedral City, Rancho Mirage, and much of Palm Desert. Beyond the dune lie the cove portions of those cities and Indian Wells and La Quinta. Farther on are the valley's first communities—Indio, Coachella, Thermal, and Mecca, and finally, the shining waters of the Salton Sea.

To the right, hugging the base of rugged Mt. San Jacinto, is Palm Springs, "playground of the stars." On the left, as you descend the grade, is Desert Hot Springs, perched atop the San Andreas fault. Heated subterranean waters come to the surface in pools now surrounded by bathhouses, hotels and mobile home parks. Just ahead are the Little San Bernardino Mountains, the western face of Joshua Tree National Park.

The view from the top of the I-10 Grade, as you approach the valley from the east, is no less spectacular. After passing through 90 miles of dry, high-desert terrain, the highway suddenly drops away before you to reveal a broad panorama of green farm-land against a backdrop of mauve mountains. On the left is the glistening blue of the Salton Sea, and ahead, on the right, San Gorgonio Pass, marked by the twin snowcapped peaks of San Gorgonio and San Jacinto. Called "The Palm of God's Hand," this beautiful valley was once the northern arm of the Gulf of California. Cut off from the sea when the Colorado River built a delta across it, through the eons it became successively an inland sea, dry land, a huge freshwater lake, and ultimately the Coachella Valley we know today. At night the unexpected sea of lights, viewed from either side of the valley, is awesome.

It's hard to believe that just over 125 years ago this was the dreaded Salton Sink—nemesis of many an overland traveler. In 1872, Southern Pacific survey parties laid out a route through the center of the valley—the last link in a southern transcontinental railroad. Not only did that railroad provide transportation into and through the desert, but the need for water for steam engines prompted extensive well drilling. Discovery of a rich underground aquifer brought settlers, drawn by the prospects of growing early fruits and vegetables, and by the health benefits of the warm, dry climate.

Coachella Valley, California—A Pictorial History tells the story of the valley's transformation from desert to one of the richest agricultural areas in the world, a world-class resort community, and home to 273,000 year-round residents. Since *Palm Springs First One Hundred Years*, written by Frank Bogert, details the history of that city, this book contains just a brief review of Palm Springs' early days. Beginning with the natural history of the Coachella Valley, its geology and Indian people, it covers all of the communities before 1920, highlights each decade to the 1950s, and takes a look at themes which affected the quality of life for the whole valley. It is hoped that the story will bring about an awareness of the debt of gratitude we owe those who literally "made the desert bloom." Their struggles and triumphs have made possible the life we enjoy here today.

Acknowledgments

Grateful recognition is given to all who have made this book possible. All of the photographs which are not individually identified in their captions have come from the Coachella Valley Historical Society's permanent collections, contributed, or actually made by Otho Moore, Ruth White Peters, Ole Nordland, A. L. Pearson, Hugh and Grace Proctor, Betty Randall Shephard, Walter Pulsifer, Robert Cook, Dewey Moore, Ray House and others. Much appreciation is due Dorothy Schmid, Geraldine Robertson, Constance Cowan, and Margaret Tyler for their identification and filing of the historic photos and memorabilia.

Others who loaned photos for inclusion are Jack Burkett, Lois Anderson, Anita Carter Ellis, the Kitagawa family, Paul Ames, Madeline Mullan, Bob and Kay Hillery, Frances Pearson, the Palm Desert Historical Society, and the Palm Springs Historical Society. Del Gagnon graciously provided the copyrighted aerial photograph of the valley today. The La Quinta Resort, PGA West, Sun City Palm Desert, the Empire Polo Club, and The Living Desert have provided the beautiful color photos.

Additionally the author was aided by Bob Walker at the Indio Library, Ann Copeland, Kathy Papan and Dennis Mahr at the Coachella Valley Water District, and by Joe Benetiz, Hazel Duro, Alice Suski, Bill Kersteiner, Harold Cousins, Ernie Dunlevie, Jeri Taylor, and Ben Laflin. Bill Johnson of Johnson Photo in Indio was most accommodating in reproducing loaned pictures.

Newspapers have been the best source of information about the early days of the valley. The earliest paper in the Coachella Valley Museum files is *The Indio Index* of 1909. A quite complete set of *The Date Palm*, Indio's weekly, and *The Coachella Valley Submarine*, published first in Thermal and then in Coachella, are rich sources of "news." They also supply real insight into the thoughts and feelings of the early-day residents. Ole Nordland, editor of Indio's *The Daily News*, had a great love of history, and the museum's collection of his clippings, from every possible source, were invaluable in researching and writing this publication.

Louisa Ames' columns entitled "Do You Remember?" were read avidly when they appeared in *The Daily News*. Paul Wilhelm's feature articles about the natural history of the area were equally popular. Dr. Ralph Pawley spent years listening to, and recording oral histories, and writing of his own first-hand experiences growing up in the valley and becoming one of its foremost physicians. His unpublished work filled in many details.

The Coachella Valley Historical Society has published the *Periscope* every year since 1978. Individual bibliographies validate the contents, relied upon by this author to present an overview of Coachella Valley history. There is much more to be told. President Arthur P. LaLonde and the Board of Directors are to be thanked for their support of this project which puts a broad span of the valley's early history into book form.

Part I—The Setting

Tufa, the solids left behind when water evaporated, was used for Indian petroglyphs.

Coachella Valley

Coachella Valley's Geography

The story of the Coachella Valley begins with the formation of a great shallow depression, or basin, which modern explorers have called the Salton Sink. Many millions of years before that, a long arm of the Pacific Ocean extended from the Gulf of California through the present Imperial and Coachella Valleys, then northwesterly through central California. Mountain ranges rose on either side of this great arm of the sea, and the whole area came up out of the water. Oyster beds in the San Felipe Mountains, on the west side of Imperial Valley are located many hundreds of feet above present sea level. Slowly the land in the center settled, and the area south of San Gorgonio Pass sloped gradually down to the gulf.

This new land area was shaped by the mighty San Andreas fault near the base of its eastern mountains and by a series of fault lines at the base of its western mountains. The eastern escarpment of Mt. San Jacinto is one of the steepest in the world, for the mountain rises 10,000 feet directly above the city of Palm Springs, whose elevation is only 466 feet. The lowest part of the depression has an elevation of 276.5 feet below sea level. Approximately 11,000 years ago it held ancient Lake Cahuilla. Carbon dioxide wells, bubbling mud pots, thermal wells, and outcroppings of obsidian and pumice attest today to the seismic activity, past and present, to be found in the valley. It has become a living textbook for geology students.

If it had not been affected by external forces, this new valley, 15 to 30 miles wide and 120 miles long, would probably have kept its original contours. However, just over those eastern mountains was one of the mightiest rivers of the North American continent—the Colorado. Its watershed covers 260,000 square miles, from the southern edge of Yellowstone Park to the Gulf of California. The river carved out the Grand Canyon, and deposited the silt at its mouth. Over the eons, it built a delta across what is now called the Gulf of California, turning the area to the north into a great saltwater lake which covered almost 2,100 square miles.

The Colorado River then chose for itself a new route on the southeastern side of the delta plain, discharging its waters into the Gulf of California. Under the blazing sun, water in the upper gulf evaporated, leaving an arid basin encrusted with salt in its deeper parts. How long this ancient sea-bottom remained dry cannot be determined, but many thousands of years ago, the Colorado River proceeded to refill the dry basin. The river, running over the raised delta plain which sloped both ways, could easily be diverted to either side. In its prehistoric floods, it often changed course, leaving the gulf and pouring its waters into the dry basin of the Salton Sink. When it had refilled the basin, and transformed it into a great freshwater lake, it broke through its silt dam and found a new outlet to the gulf. Probably for centuries, the Colorado made

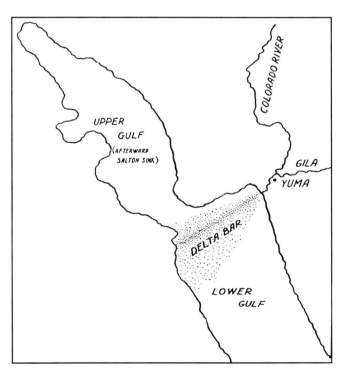

The ancient Gulf of California extended north through the present Imperial and Coachella Valleys

Ancient Lake Cahuilla's shore line is approximately forty feet above sea level. (Courtesy of Coachella Valley Water District)

the Salton Sink a freshwater lake, depositing in the process 150,000,000 tons or more of silt every year. Artesian borings at Holtville in 1913 showed sedimentary deposits in that part of Imperial Valley are more than 1,000 feet in depth. In all probability the Colorado flowed into the Salton Sink every four or five hundred years.

For three centuries or more, from 1540 to 1905, the Salton Sink was a hot, arid desert. Neither Melchior Diaz in 1540, nor Juan Bautista de Anza, who crossed it in 1774, saw anything similar to a body of water.

In 1853, Secretary of War Jefferson Davis prevailed upon Congress to authorize a series of explorations for the discovery of a practical railroad route to the Pacific Coast. Lieutenant R. S. Williamson, of the U.S. Topographic Engineers, was selected to lead the southern expedition, accompanied by a young geologist, Professor William P. Blake. Blake was the first to explain the origin of the Salton Sink, to trace its ancient history, and to give a name to the great freshwater lake it had once held. The Williamson/Blake party went down through the San Gorgonio Pass to the Coachella Valley. Following a path along the base of the mountains on the west side of the valley, Blake noticed the mark of the ancient sea which once filled the basin.

What was deposited on the rocks is not coral but tufa—solids left behind on the rocks as the water evaporated. Considering this, the thousands of shells of old sea organisms, the slope of the land toward what is now the Salton Sea, and the reading of his barometer, Blake made the assertion that this was indeed an ancient sea bottom and that it was below sea level—probably 271 feet below at its lowest point.

Blake was aided in his findings by the Cahuilla Indians in the villages he visited—Indians who told him that their ancestors had once lived in the canyons above the sea and that they came to the sea to catch fish, ducks, geese, and small animals. Then the sea had receded "poco a poco" (little by little). Once, they said, it came back in a rush, suggesting that they had experienced an overflow of the Colorado River through the New River or other channels—overflows that were still taking place within the memory of Indian ancestors. Blake noticed that the Cahuilla Indians were raising crops of corn, barley, and vegetables, using ditch irrigation to bring water from springs around the valley. He suggested in his report the possibility of irrigating this "Death Valley," possibly with water brought in channels from the Colorado River. He said, "With water, it is probable that the greater part of the desert could be made to yield crops of almost any kind." Reclamation of the desert was a bold and original idea in 1857. His accurate scientific mind could see that the sedimentary deposits needed only water to make them fertile.

It is estimated that between 1849 and 1860 eight thousand emigrants crossed the Colorado Desert on their way to California. One of these travelers, Dr. Oliver M. Wozencraft, a prominent San Francisco physician, seemed most impressed with the agricultural possibilities of the Salton Sink and the chance of irrigating it with Colorado River water. With the complete cooperation of the California legislature in 1859, he boldly asked Congress to give the state 6,000,000 acres, including the entire Coachella Valley and land in the surrounding mountains. The state would then convey all rights to the tract to Wozencraft, conditioned on his developing an irrigation system to water it.

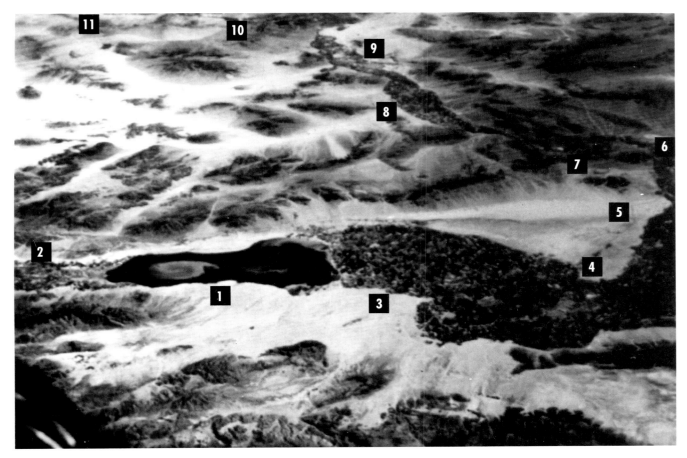

Congress ruled out almost half of the requested land, pointing out that land in the San Bernardino, Orocopia, Chocolate, and other mountains was far too high to be irrigated by Colorado River water and might have mineral value. As for the remaining 3,000,000 acres, most agreed that the land was not only worthless without irrigation, but was an impediment to travel. Newspapers wrote that they saw no obstacle to the success of the plan except the porous nature of the sand. "By removing the sand from the desert, success would be assured," they wrote. Wozencraft believed Congress was ready to make the grant when the Civil War turned attention elsewhere. Another traveler, Dr. Joseph Widney, advocated deliberately turning the Colorado River into the Salton Basin to recreate Lake Cahuilla. His plan became known as the Widney Sea idea. Obviously most of the land would be submerged if the Widney Sea was created, and Congress didn't think that made sense. Wozencraft continued to advocate his proposal until 1887, when he died, confident he was on the verge of success. In 1891, without the land grant, private enterprise made a serious attempt to realize the "dream" of turning water into the Salton Sink and creating a fertile oasis in the heart of the Colorado Desert.

This spectacular 1965 panorama was taken by Astronauts Cooper and Conrad from a height of 125 miles. Identified locations are: (1) Salton Sea; (2) Coachella Valley; (3) Imperial Valley; (4) U.S.-Mexico Border; (5) All-American Canal; (6) Yuma; (7) Imperial Dam; (8) Palo Verde Valley; (9) Parker Indian Reservation; (10) Lake Havasu; (11) Needles. (NASA photograph, courtesy of Coachella Valley Water District)

By accident, a sea came to life in the desert. (Courtesy Coachella Valley Water District)

Coachella Valley

The Salton Sea

The Salton Sea is a man-made accident, brought about by a strange set of seemingly unrelated natural disasters, and economic and political events of the late 1890s and early 1900s.

In 1891, The California Irrigation Company was formed to attempt to carry water from the Colorado River into the Salton Sink. They hired a very capable engineer, Charles R. Rockwood, who proposed taking water from the Colorado, carrying it southward into Mexico, then around a series of sand dunes and finally north into Southern California. The route was virtually the same one the river had itself used in its hundreds of years of alternately flowing into the gulf and then into the Salton Sink. In the monetary panic of 1893, the company was forced into bankruptcy and the company's maps, records, and engineering data were turned over to Mr. Rockwood to satisfy a judgment obtained in a suit for his unpaid salary of $3,500.

Rockwood had faith in the project. He formed the California Development Company and a subsidiary Mexican company needed for permission to dig a canal through Mexico. The financial resources of both companies were largely on paper so Rockwood had to secure real capital to do the work. The proposed reclamation of an arid desert, where in the summer the thermometer went to 120 degrees in the shade, and where only two or three inches of rain fell in the course of a year, did not strike Eastern capitalists as a very promising venture. At last, however, in 1898, Mr. Rockwood secured a promise from investors in New York that they would advance the necessary funds. Two days before the papers were to have been signed, the American battleship, *Maine*, was blown up in Havana harbor. This catastrophe, together with the war that followed, put an end to negotiations.

But the irrigation plan did not fail. George and William Chaffey had successfully developed a project in Australia, where temperatures reached 125 degrees. Men worked in that dry heat without a problem, so the Chaffeys reasoned that the same would be true in the Salton Sink. George Chaffey notified Rockwood that he would finance the project and on April 3, 1900, Chaffey became president of the California Development Company. The canal was dug and on May 14, 1901, the first water flowed into the Salton Sink.

The California Development Company was only a water-selling company, so the Imperial Land Company was incorporated to attract colonists. In order not to scare off settlers and small investors by using the ominous words "desert" and "sink," they changed the name of the lower basin to "The Imperial Valley." Settlers came, mutual water companies were organized, and by April 3, 1902, 400 miles of irrigation ditches had been dug and water was available for 100,000 acres of irrigable land. Chaffey sold his shares in the company in 1902.

Settlers boated amid the brush on the new sea.

Water delivery was not dependable. Silt is the toughest matter engineers have to deal with when irrigating from a turbid stream. Before the construction of Hoover Dam, a single day's supply of water for the Imperial Valley contained enough silt to make a levee twenty feet high, twenty feet wide, and one mile long. If this silt is not dredged out or collected in settling basins, it eventually raises the beds of canals, fills the ditches, and chokes the whole irrigation system. It was difficult to keep waterways open. Furthermore, the intake wasn't deep enough to take the intended canal capacity at the low stage of the river. Mass meetings were held, the company was denounced, and lawsuits were filed by settlers.

In the late summer of 1904, it was obvious that something drastic had to be done. The financially strapped company did not have the resources to buy the dredges needed to quickly clean out the clogged canal, so they decided to cut a new intake from the river at a point four miles south of the international border, eliminating the clogged portion. Little did anyone know that the river was about to make one of its semimillenial changes in course. Had they known, they would have fortified the west bank of the river, not cut through it. The cut was completed in October 1904 and elaborate plans for a control gate were immediately forwarded to Mexico City for approval, without which they had no authority to construct a gate. Approval finally came in December 1905—a year later.

The new seashore was a great place to have a picnic.

Meanwhile, there were serious problems. In the twenty-seven years that river-flow records had been kept at Yuma, there had been only three winter floods, and never two in the same year. During the winter of 1905, however, there were two floods in February. A third flood came in March and it was obvious that it was a very unusual season. Since the river was so high, it was decided to close the lower cut and take water only through the control gate oppposite Yuma.

So much for good intentions! The original cut was sixty feet wide. A dam of pilings, brush, and sandbags was thrown across it in March, but the dam had scarcely been completed when another flood came down the Colorado and swept it away. By the middle of June the river was discharging 90,000 cubic feet of water per second; the width of the lower intake had widened from sixty feet to one hundred sixty; water was overflowing the banks of the main canal, rolling across the rich Imperial Valley farmland and accumulating in the deepest part of the sink. A new Salton Sea was forming.

Southern Pacific trains ran by on their relocated tracks and offered excursions on the sea from this pier, via boat.

During the next two years, a gigantic battle was waged between man and nature. Five attempts to close the break in 1905 failed. In 1906 another flood widened the gap and sent a wall of water ten miles wide into the Imperial Valley, threatening the towns of Calexico and Mexicali and washing away hundreds of acres of valuable farmland. When its mainline from Los Angeles to Yuma was threatened, the Southern Pacific Railroad entered the fight. Tons of brush, rock and dirt were dumped into the break, but the swirling waters washed the materials away. Time and again the Southern Pacific was forced to move its mainline tracks to higher ground. For two years the entire flow of the Colorado River rushed into the Salton Sink.

It was the Southern Pacific that ultimately funded and fought the winning battle. The railroad's president, E. H. Harriman, deserves much credit for doing what neither the California Development Company, nor the state and federal governments could or would do. One further natural disaster slowed conquest of the river. The earthquake and fire in San Francisco on April 18, 1906, meant that the 850-ton floating dredge, the "Delta," which had been ordered for spring delivery, was not sent from San Francisco until the following December.

Ole Nordland, editor of the *Indio Daily News* for many years, described the effort of the Southern Pacific in these words:

The gargantuan effort of stemming the flood tied up a network of 1,200 miles of main lines for three weeks while the SP fought to bring the river under control. The work started December 20, 1906, the day of the last exchange of telegrams (between E. H. Harriman and President Theodore Roosevelt, with the latter assuring Harriman that he would be compensated). Dispatchers sidetracked crack passenger trains to let rock trains through, while amazed passengers looked on. Rock trains came from as far away as 480 miles to hurtle 2,057 carloads of rock, 221 carloads of gravel, and 203 carloads of clay into the break in 15 days. The loads were dumped from two trestles built across the river break and were literally dumped faster than the river could wash them away. The Colorado River put up a stubborn fight. Three times it ripped away the trestle piles. But finally, on January 27, 1907, the breach was closed and the valleys' farms and cities were saved. The Colorado River was returned to its former path, but it left in its wake today's Salton Sea.

The Roby home in Mecca was built from ties salvaged from abandoned Southern Pacific tracks.

Mt. San Jacinto is framed by these ancient palms at Biskra.

Coachella Valley

The Native Palm Oases

Desert plant life is wonderfully varied. Of particular interest in Coachella Valley is the Washingtonia filifera fan palm, the only native palm in the United States. On both sides of the valley, the palms grow where earthquake fault lines have allowed water to rise to the surface. The famous San Andreas fault is clearly marked by the palm groves of the Indio Hills north and northwest of Indio—oases that are named from southeast to northwest, Metate, Curtis, Biskra, McComber, Pushawalla, Thousand Palms, and Willis Palms.

Biskra Palms is one of several oases used as movie locations.

Many of these oases have been used for movie locations. *Tripoli* and *Ten Tall Men* were filmed at Biskra Palms. *Son of the Sheik*, and DeMille's *King of Kings*, were filmed at Thousand Palms Canyon. *The Silver Chalice* was filmed at Willis Palms.

An extravagant plan for one of these oases was doomed by the stock market crash of 1929. "The Walled Oasis of Biskra," was pinpointed as "three miles north of the desert town of Indio,

California." It was supposed to feature a $500,000 hotel in the architectural style of the Sahara. Plans called for a completely walled oasis of narrow streets and alluring shops. Private estates surrounding the oasis would be built in a Near-Eastern architectural style. Everyone, including the merchants in Oriental shops, were to wear Arabian costumes with turban and fez.

Apostle Palms, shown in this 1912 photograph, was the only known palm oasis in the floor of the valley. Located near what is now Avenue 38 and Madison Street, it was the site of a stage stop before the coming of the railroad. Southern Pacific records state that it hauled water from this well to the site of Indio in 1876. The palms later burned.

A road to the oasis, long rock walls, and desert trails were built. Every weekend hundreds of visitors were driven to the oasis by bus where an enormous tent served as a dining room. Caterers were brought in from Indio to serve dinners, and camels added atmosphere. Then came the bleak news from Wall Street, ruining the hopes of the developers. The spires, domes, and towers were never to rise as stockholders of the Biskra Trust went down with the crash. Only the original walled terraces remain in mute testimony to the dream.

20

This photo shows the North Grove at Thousand Palms Oasis.

Geologists claim that the oases in the Coachella Valley are the remnants of a once great forest of palms that bordered ancient Lake Cahuilla. Before the advent of the white man, Indians found good water and shade for their homes. They harvested mesquite beans and stayed for the ripening of the palm berry, a small black coffee-seed-like fruit. At every oasis, traces of these "first people" can be found.

Paul Wilhelm, one of the valley's great naturalists, would be pleased to know how much his Thousand Palms Oasis home is enjoyed and appreciated by today's visitors to its serene environment. He wrote about the palms, "On starlit nights the palms stand out like prophets of old against the twinkling sky. As for poetry and mystery, they are both ever present among the whispering palms of any oasis you chance to visit."

Paul Wilhelm, seated in his beloved sanctuary.

The grove at Hidden Springs can be reached from a trail in Box Canyon.

The Native Palm Oases

Shatta, weaver of Cahuilla baskets, was the grandmother of Ruby Modesto who worked tirelessly in the 1960s and 1970s to pass on Cahuilla language and customs to younger generations.

The First People

Chapter Four

Who were the first human inhabitants of the land we know today as the Coachella Valley?

Ancestors of our present day Indians probably came into the valley from the east about 900 years ago, making trails from the Palo Verde Valley and the Colorado River. They lived in villages, enjoying the hot springs and cool streams that flowed into the desert from the western mountains. They fished in the great inland lake which periodically filled the basin, and made an annual migration to cooler mountain homes in the summer. They lived off the land, using desert and mountain plants for food, shelter, and medicine. They hunted rabbits, deer, sheep, and small animals and used the skins for clothing. They farmed, digging wells and irrigation ditches to water their vegetable crops.

This photo of Indian leaders includes, from left to right, in the back row, Captain Ramon, Captain Jim, and Captain Sastro, and in the front row, Captain Habiel, Captain Will Pablo, Chief Cabazon, Captain Manuel, and Captain Jose Maria.

The Desert Cahuilla were able to establish villages out in the floor of the valley with their ingenious wells. Wherever there was a seep or weak spring, they would construct a long, narrow, open passageway, with steps or a ramp leading down to the water, usually within fifteen to thirty feet of the surface. Earth was removed by carrying it in the baskets to the surface. (Courtesy of Coachella Valley Water District)

Probably there had been earlier people in the valley, part of that great migration across the Bering Sea 20,000 years ago. Some bands may well have stopped in the desert before their descendants continued south. Pinto Man lived in the Pinto Basin of Joshua Tree National Park, and artifacts dating back 10,000 years give evidence that people resided around a large freshwater lake, surrounded by lush vegetation. Bones of prehistoric camels and fossil evidence of rich plant life are found in the Indio and Mecca Mud Hills.

James and Elizabeth Moore are shown
with several of their beautiful Cahuilla
baskets.

A. L. Kroeber, in his classic work, *Handbook of the Indians of California*, lists specific tribes of both the Colorado and Mojave Deserts. He names the Cahuilla nation in the western section and east to the Yuman River territory and the Chemehuevi west of the river. The Chemehuevi were probably the most recent migrants into the Coachella Valley, their move prompted by disputes with the Yumans over lands bordering the Colorado River. Chemehuevis hunted and gathered most of their foods, but those living along the river planted and harvested crops. Credit for saving the Medjool date variety from extinction is due a Chemehuevi farmer, in one of the most interesting stories relative to the beginning of the date industry in the United States. Chemehuevi women made some of the finest baskets in all of California. Unlike other tribes, they sewed their baskets with willow and other plant fibers.

Baseball was a favorite sport in the early 1900s and many Indian young men played on valley teams. The *Coachella Valley Submarine* of September 16, 1921, carried a front-page article entitled "Jim Brothers Sail for Japan. Valley Has Two Members on Indian Ball Team Enroute to Orient." The article states that Harry and Alex Jim, two star players from a Coachella Valley Club, would be in Japan for two weeks playing teams representing leading Japanese universities. (Courtesy of Coachella Valley Water District)

In this broad region, there had been a natural intermingling of people. From 300 to 500 people lived in each village. They governed themselves in the manner of clans, with final appeal to a group Head Chief, or Net. Professor David Prescott Barrows considered the Cahuillas the most powerful and best known of all Southern California tribes. When he authored his handbook in 1923 he numbered the Cahuillas at 750, but he believed there may have been 2500 at one time. He listed three groups—Western or Pass Cahuilla, which included Palm Springs and the San Gorgonio Pass area; Desert Cahuilla from east of Palm Springs to the Salton Sea; and the Mountain Cahuilla, south of San Jacinto peak and in the Santa Rosa Mountains.

Many village sites were temporary, tied to the availability of certain seeds and plant foods and occupied only at times of harvest. The Palm Springs area was probably the easternmost site of the Western Cahuilla villages. In some ways the village at Indian

This 1915 photograph shows how Indians stored mesquite beans, seeds, and other provisions in these huge off-the-ground baskets of woven weeds and mud.

Wells seemed tied to both the Western and Desert Cahuilla, but the wells they dug would indicate they were probably Desert Cahuilla. These desert dwellers lived on the floor of the Colorado Desert, often near the palm oases at the base of the Indio and Mecca Hills where the San Andreas fault line allowed water to rise to the surface and provide a permanent water supply.

Probably the most important Desert Cahuilla village was the one called Puichekiva (Road Runner's House), located about seven miles south of Coachella. There, a good well furnished a reliable supply of domestic water. From time to time remnants of clans from the Santa Rosa Mountain villages came here. There were a number of family dwellings in this village which boasted two ceremonial houses. The village at Torres was dominated by two clans and each of their Nets owned ceremonial houses there.

At a site about five miles northeast of Mecca, at Painted Canyon, there were twelve houses belonging to the clan of Chief Cabazon. The Indian name for that village meant "The Place Where the Ceremonial Mats Are Spread." The name was significant, for Cabazon was for many years the spokesman, leader, and ceremonial Net for many of the Cahuilla villages. It has been claimed that authorities in power in California had given him authority over all the Cahuilla and Serrano Indians of the desert, and over all native peoples from San Gorgonio Pass to Los Angeles. Desert Cahuilla villages united under Cabazon may well have been the beginnings of a genuine tribal organization. When

The County of Riverside erected this historical marker near the end of Jackson Street and Avenue 66 to mark interesting, but still unexplained, rock formations which may have been fish traps.

Cabazon died, his son succeeded him, but by then the white man's civilization was taking its toll on tribal life and the Desert Cahuilla became dwellers on their separate reservations—the Torres-Martinez Reservation, northwest of the Salton Sea; the Augustine Reservation in the center of the valley near Coachella Valley High School; and the Cabazon Reservation just east of Indio. The Indians of the Palm Springs area, with close ties to the Desert Cahuilla, became dwellers on the Agua Caliente Reservation. In 1976, a division of the Cabazon Reservation gave land rights to Chemehuevi Indians whose principal reservation at Twenty Nine Palms had been reduced and its boundaries realigned.

These views of buildings on the Torres-Martinez Reservation were taken in the 1950s.

Coachella Valley

The end of the old way of life for the Indians of the Coachella Valley came in 1877. The railroad had been completed—alternate sections of land had been given to the Southern Pacific Company and settlers came in ever increasing numbers. Indians needed employment when their traditional lands were taken away, and they could no longer live by hunting and gathering. They became the backbone of the work force in the building of the railroad, the operation of the salt works in the Salton Sink, and in farming.

Fig Tree John, wearing his dress uniform, is shown with his grandchildren and his wife outside their home at the north end of the Salton Sea. She, like other valley wives, spent summers in the cooler climate of Banning, staying with relatives on the Morongo Reservation.

The years 1926 and 1927 saw the passing of two Cahuilla men, Juanito Razon (better known as Fig Tree John) and Ambrosio Costillo, who gained fame within the white as well as the Indian communities of the Coachella Valley. Ambrosio, a tribal medicine man, became a great help to Dr. June Robertson, BIA doctor to the valley reservations. In 1908, when an epidemic of seventy-eight cases of measles broke out among Indian families, Ambrosio worked day and night administering the white doctor's medicine and enforcing the quarantine. He was famous as a "fire eater" and performed at fiestas and the earliest Festival of Dates. *The Date Palm* newspaper of October 8, 1926, included these words of tribute, "Ambrosio Costillo, one of our best known Indians, passed away at the ripe old age of about 75 years. . . . Be it remembered that he had the respect of all who knew him. He was buried on the Toro reservation where he had lived so long. The funeral was attended by hundreds of Indians and whites."

The *Coachella Valley Submarine* of April 15, 1927, carried the news of the death of Fig Tree John at age 136, calling him "probably the most picturesque character in all the Indian tribes of the Southwest." He was said to have served as a scout for John C. Fremont's expedition through the Coachella Valley in 1842, and

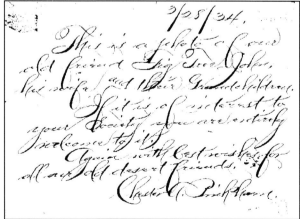

This is the hand-written note from Chester Pinkham who sent the photograph to the Historical Society.

This 1905 photograph of Fig Tree John's jacal includes a view of his buggy. It was a familiar sight at valley celebrations for he and his wife were popular participants. He was known as a good horse trader and often provided mounts for early-day travelers through the area.

he claimed to have been one of a band of Indians who helped Kearney's troops win the Battle of San Pasqual on December 6, 1846. On trips to Mecca, Thermal, or Coachella for supplies he was said to pay with gold, a practice which led people to surmise that he had a claim somewhere in the mountains west of the sea. His obituary mentions that his last public appearance was September 9, 1926, when he was taken to Riverside as a guest of honor at the unveiling of a tablet placed in memory of John Fremont and Luis Rubidoux.

Captain Jim and Jesse Rice Pearson were typical of settlers and Indians who worked together to make the valley grow.

Part II–The Early Days of Settlement—1870s to 1920

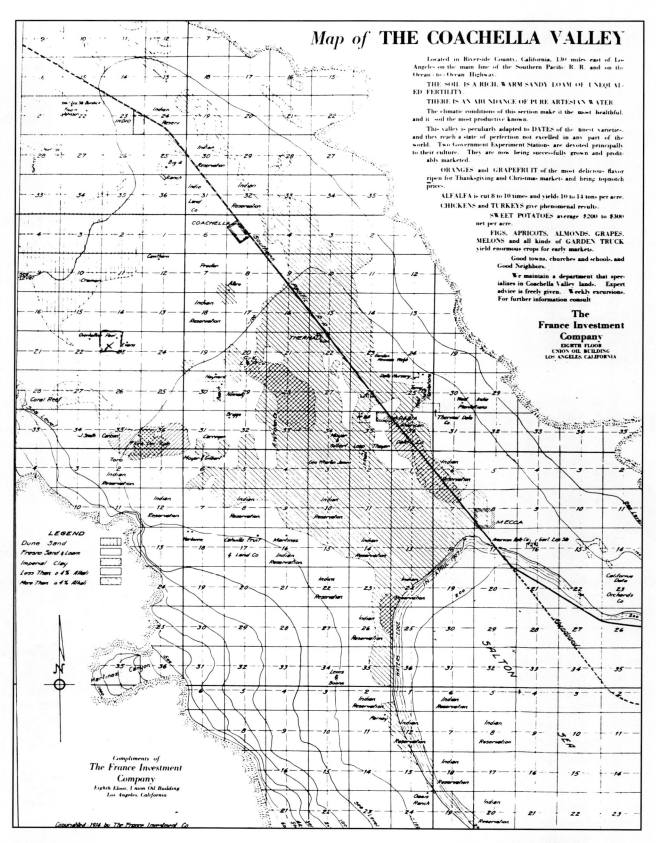

Map of THE COACHELLA VALLEY

Located in Riverside County, California, 130 miles east of Los Angeles on the main line of the Southern Pacific R. R. and on the Ocean-to-Ocean Highway.

THE SOIL IS A RICH, WARM SANDY LOAM OF UNEQUAL-ED FERTILITY.

THERE IS AN ABUNDANCE OF PURE ARTESIAN WATER

The climatic conditions of this section make it the most healthful, and it soil the most productive known.

This valley is peculiarly adapted to DATES of the finest varieties, and they reach a state of perfection not excelled in any part of the world. Two Government Experiment Stations are devoted principally to their culture. They are now being successfully grown and profit-ably marketed.

ORANGES and GRAPEFRUIT of the most delicious flavor ripen for Thanksgiving and Christmas markets and bring topnotch prices.

ALFALFA is cut 8 to 10 times and yields 10 to 14 tons per acre.

CHICKENS and TURKEYS give phenomenal results.

SWEET POTATOES average $200 to $300 net per acre.

FIGS. APRICOTS. ALMONDS. GRAPES. MELONS and all kinds of GARDEN TRUCK yield enormous crops for early markets.

Good towns, churches and schools, and Good Neighbors.

We maintain a department that spec-ializes in Coachella Valley lands. Expert advice is freely given. Weekly excursions. For further information consult

The France Investment Company
EIGHTH FLOOR
UNION OIL BUILDING
LOS ANGELES, CALIFORNIA

LEGEND
Dune Sand
Fresno Sand & Loam
Imperial Clay
Less Than 0.1% Alkali
More Than 0.1% Alkali

Compliments of
The France Investment Company
Eighth Floor, Union Oil Building
Los Angeles, California

Copyrighted 1914 by The France Investment Co.

This 1914 map shows how closely development hugged the railroad. Note the town of Arabia, and the abandoned tracks in the Salton Sea.
(Courtesy of the Laflin family and Coachella Valley Water District)

Partners in the Early Days—
The Railroad and Agriculture

One of the great sagas of the Old West took place in the twentieth century. It was the transformation of the Salton Basin into the rich winter gardens, date groves, and fabulous resort and vacation centers of the Coachella Valley. In the days of the California Gold Rush, the Salton Basin was the dreaded obstacle of the Southern Route to the Pacific. Men and wagon trains survived all the other grim hazards of the long trek, only to lose their lives or their possessions on its 100 miles of desolation. But the basin was never a sterile desert. It was filled with rich, soft silt—the top soil deposited by the Colorado River. It was a desert only because it lacked water.

This horse-drawn cook wagon served the crews surveying for the railroad route through the valley. Photograph circa 1872. (Courtesy of Coachella Valley Water District)

Enter the railroad! In its early days the Coachella Valley was probably more affected by those two steel rails than any other material feature. Behind those chugging locomotives there followed the farmer, the merchant, the miner and all those who filled the empty lands and "made the desert bloom." Presently, we take trains for granted, but it was not until March 1872 that the Southern Pacific Railroad Survey Party located its center line through the valley. They chose a route passing through the present site of Indio, near an old location designated as "Indian Wells."

Building and maintaining the tracks through the desert was not easy. Frequent cloudbursts washed out the newly graded route. Culverts and rip-rap of rocks were necessary to protect the grade from the floods of the canyons. A new hazard confronted the crews—"blow sand." In the center of the sandy areas it was necessary to build a siding known as "Saliva." It was also necessary to maintain a section crew to shovel out sand which covered the tracks and filled switches. Sharp sand particles would cut off telegraph poles very quickly. The crews laid rails to Edom, just south of the present site of Thousand Palms, then on to Myoma, west of the present railroad overpass, and finally into Indio.

This is the Southern Pacific Depot Clubhouse and Restaurant, about 1900. Crews had sleeping quarters above and passengers were served meals below. Built about 1880, the depot was the social center of Indio during its early years.

Searching for possible problems along the tracks was done by a crew using this 1903 Inspection Car and Coach.

Indio was an ideal location for a division point for it was not only halfway to Yuma from Los Angeles, but it was near an Indian reservation, where labor was available. The first trains were scheduled out of Indio to Los Angeles on May 29, 1876, and they ran on Mondays, Wednesdays, and Fridays.

Otho Moore's 1905 photograph shows the original six-stall roundhouse.

A 1907 view of the rail yard looking south from the depot. Passenger trains provided transportation between Indio, Coachella, Thermal, and Mecca, much like local bus service today. The "Sidewinder" often took partygoers home to Indio from a dance in Thermal.

Southern Pacific officials learned that the Santa Fe was nearing the Colorado River near Needles and officials determined to make every effort to reach Yuma as soon as possible. A townsite was proposed. Living quarters were erected for train crews and railroad workers. A restaurant was open twenty-four hours a day.

Above: In 1907, children of the operators of the Southern Pacific Hotel enjoyed its garden on the east side of the building.

Left: Southern Pacific workers' cottages were located between the tracks and Indio Boulevard.

While the first crews finished the work of building structures at Indio, rail-laying crews had gone on toward Walters (Mecca), building a siding at Woodspur (Coachella) and a stop at Thermal, and by January 1877 they were speeding on toward the Colorado River, which they reached and bridged on September 30, 1877. Crews from the East met them there.

This 1912 photograph shows "Fast Passenger Engine 3033" in the Indio Southern Pacific yards. It was the fastest engine in the Southern Pacific fleet, rated at 83 miles per hour.

In 1915, Ben Laflin (with dog) was happy to have this artesian well on his ranch south of Thermal. Artesian pressure sent the water ten feet in the air.

Bernard Johnson planted these imported offshoots in Mecca in 1904.

Paul Popenoe traveled across the Middle East and North Africa in 1912 to secure thousands of date offshoots for U.S. growers.

Steam engines needed water, and reliable wells were essential. In 1894, at Mecca, well drillers hit a gusher of artesian water. A trestle was built and a long pipe placed atop the trestle, with water valves spaced every car length. The westbound trains set out empty cars and the eastbound trains would pick up full cars en route to Yuma. Ten tank cars could be filled at a time, by artesian pressure. A telegraph station was established at Walters and the operator was responsible for filling the empty cars as well as handling train orders. In the days before electricity, water that flowed, even gushed, from the ground seemed like a miracle. The transformation from barren desert to lush green fields was about to become a reality.

Brief mention should be made of the rail rate war of 1887, when passenger fares from the Missouri River to the Pacific Coast were slashed to $1! From 1888 through 1891, the Southern Pacific sent five-car special trains throughout the Midwest with exhibits of California produce to attract home seekers.

Date offshoots were loaded at Bagdad for shipment to the U.S.

The publicity was unrealistically encouraging. Fruits and vegetables were the first crops planted in the Coachella Valley. Then, as now, if one crop was a big moneymaker, everyone planted it the next year and over-supply ruined the market. People became rich and went broke on onions, melons, and even cotton. An exotic crop, dates, was expected to turn growers into millionaires overnight, albiet they had to wait four or five years for a crop, and often years to acquire offshoots of good commercial varieties. The local Indio newspaper, *The Date Palm*, carried front-page articles about each new importation of date palm offshoots, and the prices received for the first pounds of dates they produced.

Dates produced on trees grown from seed are never true to the parent variety and seldom are of commercial quality. Therefore, just before the turn of the century, a young agricultural explorer, Dr. Walter T. Swingle, was sent by the United States Department of Agriculture to Algeria to study date culture and to import offshoots of the better commercial varieties for trial in the

American Southwest. In 1901 and 1902 importations were made from Egypt and the Persian Gulf areas. Dr. Swingle had concluded that the Salton Basin was the most promising area in the U.S. for date culture. Dates require high summer temperatures, plenty of water, and no rain at the time of ripening. Largely because of these early importations and Dr. Swingle's studies, the USDA began an experimental date garden near Mecca in 1904. Most of the work was moved to Indio in 1907.

This 1913 exhibit at the county fair in Riverside featured dates.

The railroad carried the produce of the farms to market. Labor was supplied by the Indians already living in the area and by Mexican families drawn to the developing ranches. From 1903 on, all manner of settlers came—those sent by doctors to find a warm, dry climate and those looking for a new frontier. The challenge appealed to men and to some hardy women, but it was no paradise. The settlers of the Coachella Valley fought sun, wind, sand, dust, and most of all, unending summer heat. Men dreamed of green fields and profitable harvests. Women endured the hardships to make homes, bear children, teach school, care for the sick, and bring a sense of beauty and culture to this arid land, and to work in the fields alongside the men.

Typical of these settlers were the Japanese men, and later their families, who moved into the valley in horse-drawn wagons, lured by the prospects of growing early spring vegetables. First to arrive was Frank T. Sakemi, in 1903, followed by Kanjiro Sakemi and Toyoichi Shibata in 1906, and Asauemon "Joe" Kitagawa in 1912. The story of the Kitagawa family reveals the kind of contribution these Japanese families made to the development of the valley.

Orphaned in Japan, Joe arrived in San Francisco in 1903. He migrated south and picked oranges in Riverside. He learned

This view of the *Yost Ranch* shows Leland Yost and Joe Kitagawa (on right), with the grape crew.

The Kitagawa family in 1929 (left to right): Kikuye, Koto, Yeichi, George, Joe, and Yeji. (Courtesy of the Kitagawa family)

The Kitagawa family in 1929 (left to right): Kikuye, Koto, Yeichi, George, Joe, and Yeji. (Courtesy of the Kitagawa family)

English quickly and made new American friends. In 1912, he traveled to the Coachella Valley, found work on a farm, and saved his earnings. In 1914 he returned to Japan and married Koto Nishimura. Together they came to the Coachella Valley and worked on the Leland Yost farm. They lived in Coachella, where a son and daughter were born.

In 1919 Joe and Koto returned to Japan to build a house, as promised, for Koto's mother. Koto and their children stayed in Japan for a year while the house was being built and Joe returned by himself to continue working in the Coachella Valley. Koto and her daughter returned to California, leaving her son to live with his grandmother, and Koto and Joe began sharecropping with Howard Carr, growing tomatoes.

With a growing family and a successful tomato crop, Joe and Koto purchased their first farm in Oasis, on Highway 86 and Avenue 76, across from the Oasis Elementary School which, at that time, was a one-room country school. They grew dates and vegetables. Their oldest son returned from Japan to join the family which, by then, numbered seven children. These were busy times and all the children were expected to work on the farm before and after school.

In 1940 the Kitagawas gathered for a family photograph including (left to right): Kikuye, Koto, Yeichi, Mary, George, Toshiko, Yeji, Jack, and Joe. (Courtesy of the Kitagawa family)

The Japanese community grew. There was a Japanese Christian Church on Avenue 50 in Coachella and "Japanese School" was held on Saturdays to teach the children their culture and language. All were expected to become proficient in English in regular public school classrooms. One mother even accompanied her first grade son to Lucy Laflin's class in Thermal so that she, too, could learn English.

On New Year's Day, following the bombing of Pearl Harbor, authorities arrived at the Kitagawa home. Joe was considered a leader among the Japanese community and he was taken to the Riverside County Jail for questioning. He was incarcerated and eventually transported to an internment camp in Missoula, Montana, in 1942. The change in climate, from the desert heat to the Montana winter, affected Joe's health and he never fully recovered from the experience.

On February 19, 1942, President Roosevelt signed Executive Order 9066 which authorized the relocation of more than 100,000 Japanese. Both American citizens and immigrants were evacuated to internment camps. The Kitagawas were forced to leave their home in the Coachella Valley on July 8, 1942. They were sent to an internment camp in Posten, Arizona. Mr. Arthur Westerfield, president of the First National Bank in Coachella, agreed to look after the ranch for the Kitagawas. In 1943, Joe was reunited with his family in Poston, and, during his internment there, he worked as a farm manager overseeing the growing of crops for the camp.

At the end of World War II, Joe, Koto, and the rest of the family returned to the Coachella Valley. Five years later the four brothers decided to farm independently. Joe divided the farmland among his sons. Joe and his youngest son Jack continued to farm the date ranch. Yechi and George chose to farm one of the existing vegetable ranches, and Yeji farmed a forty-acre parcel of vegetable land on his own.

Eventually Joe and Koto sold their Oasis date farm and retired, living their remaining years in an adobe house located on Yeji's property, enjoying their nineteen grandchildren. Joe passed away on July 21, 1970, at the age of eighty-three, followed by Koto on May 4, 1981, at the age of eighty-seven. Currently Kiyoko and her oldest son, Joe, still farm land which includes the original forty acres—a family saga spanning almost the entire history of farming in the Coachella Valley.

Joe and Koto Kitagawa cut their cake in celebration of their Fiftieth Wedding Anniversary in 1964. (Courtesy of the Kitagawa family)

Family farms characterized Coachella Valley agriculture for many years. Mexican as well as Anglo families worked together to make the desert bloom. Three generations of the Ames family have been leaders in agricultural development. Paul Ames (on right) brought national recognition to Coachella Valley in 1958 when he was recognized as one of four "Outstanding Young Farmers of the USA." (Courtesy of Paul Ames)

Mr. A. G. Tingman, shown here with his wife, is known as the "Father of Indio." He came as a railroad construction boss in 1877 and became telegrapher and station agent in 1883. He built Indio's first store northwest of the depot in 1885 and became Indio's first postmaster July 3, 1888. He homesteaded and purchased 160 acres in 1891 and laid out the original townsite, drilled a well for his home and store, and built a corral for travelers, prospectors, and freighters. In 1903 he sold his store and devoted himself to mining until his death at the Full Moon Mine, north of Niland, in 1925. (Courtesy of Coachella Valley Water District)

The First Communities

Chapter Six

Indio

Indio had its beginnings as a railroad town. The Southern Pacific–Central Pacific Illustrated Tourist's Guide of 1883 stated, "ALL TRAINS STOP at the HOTEL at INDIO, and passengers going EAST and WEST get Dinner, and have 25 minutes for the same. The Hotel at Indio is 100 feet below sea level." Trains would telegraph ahead to let the hotel cook know how many meals to prepare, reporting the information from Mecca in the east and Edom in the west. By the time the train pulled in, the meals were served and consumed in the allotted time.

The Southern Pacific Hotel and related facilities were the focal point of life. Most of the town's first inhabitants worked for the railroad, but its trains brought in settlers—those seeking relief from respiratory diseases; those seeing the opportunity of making a living serving the railroad workers; and those optimistic about the prospects for farming. The story of Indio is a story of how communities come into being. Reading early newspapers, one can sense the flavor of life here—

before towns were incorporated,

before water systems, telephones, and electricity were in place,

before paved roads connected communities and homes,

before paid firemen took care of all manner of emergencies,

before there were hospitals,

and you realize that a decent life depended on ordinary people doing extraordinary things to care for one another.

Fires were particularly dangerous. The fire hose from the SP Station was the only protection available for those first houses and stores. An article in *The Indio Index* of January 26, 1909, stated that the Indio Volunteer Fire Department had been called out twice in the prior week and that it was fortunate that the one thousand feet of SP fire hose was adequate to reach both conflagrations. As Indio grew, however, it was to "rely on the bucket brigade" or "watch it burn." It would have been useless to buy a fire truck when there were no underground pipe lines to carry water to fire hydrants. Both Indio and Coachella purchased chemical fire carts, but they were only effective if firefighters could get to a fire in its early stages. Most structures were built of flammable materials and burned quickly.

Then there was the matter of trained personnel. Every fire department in the valley began as a volunteer fire department. Civic-minded citizens voluntarily made themselves available to be trained as firefighters, and committed themselves to be available when fires occurred. There was a fondness expressed toward "the fire boys" or the "fire laddies" as the papers often called them.

Lack of good medical facilities often meant death to those unfortunate enought to be badly burned. Victims were given emergency treatment and put on the next west-bound train for follow-up care. Chapter 13 gives a picture of the beginnings of valley health care.

When miners began arriving on their way to hoped-for riches in the mountains east of Indio, they stopped for provisions and loaded their mules in this corral behind Tingman's store.

Many settlers came by covered wagon. Edith Mann Ross, who arrived in Indio in 1896, remembered walking beside her family's wagon on the trip from Vancouver, Washington, to the desert. Shown is the Ross Homestead with Bailey, Edith's future husband, and his parents.

Indio's first school building was built in 1898 and served as a community center and on Sunday as a church. The bell was donated by the railroad.

Howard Gard, second from left, stands in front of his store at the corner of Fargo and Miles Avenue in 1903.

Constables used this building made of railroad ties to house suspected criminals until swift justice could be dispensed. There was no roof, running water, or toilet. Local restaurants prepared the food. Pioneers pointed out that crime was rare.

This 1913 photograph shows three Courtney daughters and David Elgin. All were born in Indio in the late 1890s and early 1900s.

Coachella Valley

This tent house in Indio was typical of most "first homes" in 1907.

An eight-mule team pulled this freighting wagon to the rear of H. E. Tallent's Store in 1909.

This view of the north side of Fargo Street about 1915 shows Wrang Lumber, the Green Hotel, and the first school building in the background.

The home of Chester Sparey was built in 1915 near Avenue 42 and Jackson Street. Sparey was one of those farsighted men who helped spearhead the effort which led to the establishment of the Coachella Valley County Water District.

Warm rains and melting snow brought mile-wide torrents of water through Indio on January 18, 1916, as shown in this view of Fargo Street. The flood provided the impetus to hasten efforts to build new channels east of Point Happy.

In 1920 a lot at the corner of Jackson and Requa Streets was purchased for the Indio Methodist Church, which had been meeting in a school building. This building became the church home until construction of the new church at Requa and Deglet Noor.

The depot at Coachella was the center of activity for the town.

Coachella

Shortly after the railroad was constructed through Coachella Valley, a depot and siding were constructed at a site south of Indio, aptly named "Woodspur." The area was forested with mesquite trees and the railroad contracted with the Indians for wood for its locomotives.

Jack Holliday, a well driller from Norwalk, visited Woodspur in 1896 and found a small agricultural experiment station, sponsored by the Southern Pacific. A twelve-inch well seeped a little water. In 1898 Holliday returned to the valley with a rotary hydraulic well-drilling rig and put down a well near present Vine and Third Streets. He installed a wooden water tank on a tower for a gravity-flow system, then installed water mains for the town. Development was assured. Bill Kersteiner, in a 1998 interview, recalled that the ground under the tank was always damp and it was a great source of earthworms for fishing.

In 1901, a Land and Water Company was formed for the development of the Woodspur townsite. I. H. Faye, manager of the company, hired J. L. Rector, a surveyor, to lay out the townsite. The name Woodspur did not strike Mr. Faye as an appealing name. In 1901 a general meeting of all those interested in a name change was called. Seventeen men responded. Jack Holliday recalled what happened in these words, "After much consideration, it was decided to use parts of two names, *Cahuilla*, the tribal name for the local Indians, and *concha*, which referred to the multitude of small sea shells found in the valley sand, to form a new name, *Coachella*, for the developing village. At this meeting it was decided to change the name of *Cahuilla Valley* to *Coachella Valley*.

Mesquite groves, which covered much of the valley, are shown in this view of the Burnett camp. Land was being cleared for farming.

E. N. T. Burnett wrote on this photograph, "Fred, Paul and I loading 65,860 pounds of mesquite which we hauled from my farm and sold for firewood to an LA firm."

This horse-drawn steam well-drill outfit is shown in front of the Coachella depot.

Mrs. Charles McDonald organized the first Sunday school in her home in 1902.

"The U.S. Government Postal Service accepted these name changes and established the new post office cubical in George Huntington's store with George becoming the first Postmaster of Coachella on November 30, 1901."

There are other theories as to the origin of the name, Coachella, but the meeting of settlers seems to be the most plausible. The U.S. Geological Survey reports that the name was officially approved at a meeting of the Board on Geographic Names on January 6, 1909.

Mr. and Mrs. Charles McDonald arrived in 1901 and McDonald purchased lots for $50 each on Front Street and also on the north side of the present day Seventh Street. McDonald built a tent house as living quarters for his family behind the proposed site for his General Store, which he built in 1902 with partner, Manny Young. He sold everything—groceries, dry goods, hardware, seed, cattle feed, lumber, and building materials. A cold storage for meat was located in the basement. There was no electricity or refrigeration, and ice was obtained from Colton via the railroad. In 1905 McDonald began building a cement block building around the frame structure, and on its completion, the original building was removed.

McDonald was a good carpenter and he built the first schools, and, in 1907, the Presbyterian Church. It was the first

Charles McDonald built the Presbyterian Church in 1907.

Charles McDonald also built a second, larger school on the site of the present Palm View School.

mainline valley church, chartered in 1902. The first minister, Albert Dilworth, was the father of Nelson Dilworth, who later became a California state senator.

Dave Thomas with his oldest daughter, Blanche, to cook and keep house for him, came to Coachella from Nebraska in 1901. Early in 1902, he purchased land with artesian water near town. His wife, Matilda, with children Aurel, Ralph, and Eva came with a team of horses, cow, chickens, and farm implements by "mixed train" of box cars and passenger cars. The family cared for the livestock whenever the train made a stop and had fresh milk to drink all the way to California.

John and Lucy Smythe bought a half interest in the Huntington Store around 1909. Lucy was from Atlanta. Her twin sister was married to a Coca-Cola Company executive—a connection that undoubtedly gave the Smythes good information on setting up the Smythe Bottling Plant. School children remembered with pleasure their free drinks after a tour of the plant. Smythes ultimately bought out Huntington.

A disastrous fire struck the business district and all but the cement block buildings were destroyed. McDonald thought it was

time for Coachella to have a bank so in one of the new cement-block buildings, he included a large cement vault. Harry Westerfield came from Banning to open the First National Bank of Coachella in 1912.

As rebuilding progressed, stores came into being on Broadway, west of Front Street, including a Masonic Hall, theater, drug store, a hardware store, pool hall, barber shop, then a two-story building with offices upstairs and Lyle Pearson's store downstairs, and finally the new First National Bank. Mr. Pearson's hobby was photography and his pictures are an invaluable record of what those early days were like.

Coachella was built by many public-spirited citizens. One was Fred Zabler, an attorney who was told that his wife's severe rheumatoid arthritis would benefit from the valley's climate. Zablers came in 1910, living first in a tent house, then adding rooms around it. Fred became the first insurance agent in the valley, was active in the Presbyterian Church and served for many years on the school board. After school closed, Fred would inspect the school property for necessary repairs. On finding scratched desks, he would have his children sand and varnish them.

Originally electrical power was limited to generators powered by diesel engines. Two small local companies were replaced by Southern Sierra Power Company, and, in 1914, lines were built from San Bernardino to Redlands and on into the Coachella and Imperial Valleys. Their main distribution plant was in Coachella. The power company furnished a mile of line and a transformer to each farmer using fifteen or more horsepower. Feeder lines were built from Coachella to the towns and

Left: Coachella residents celebrated Christmas 1909 on Broadway, the town's main street.

This 1909 photograph of the Huntington and Smythe Store used its buildings as the first billboard in Coachella, advertising the area as "Earliest fruit and vegetable land in California."

J. L. Rector's billboard was plainly visible to passengers on trains as they sped through Coachella, not only advertising land but telling travelers that they were seventy-six feet below sea level.

The Coachella Pool Hall was a popular gathering place.

ranches of the valley. Caleb Cook, F. M. Runyen and others electrically inclined were busy first wiring the stores and then the homes for electric lights and power-driven machines. The hardware stores of the valley began stocking electric wire, insulators, switches, plugs, lighting fixtures, electric fans, and appliances. Coachella's location in the center of the valley positioned it to be a main commercial center.

This photograph of the Kelly and Rouff Blacksmith Shop shows the varied nature of the business—horseshoeing and repairing the automobiles that became more numerous after 1910.

Henry and Margaret McKay peddled meat from this 1913 Chevrolet. In 1914 they suffered the loss of their only son in a fire caused by an exploding oil stove—a common accident in the valley's early days.

This 1914 photograph of Coachella's main street shows the original office of the First National Bank. (Courtesy of Coachella Valley Water District)

Ralph Thomas and A. L. Pearson stand on the steps of their store which opened February 6, 1917.

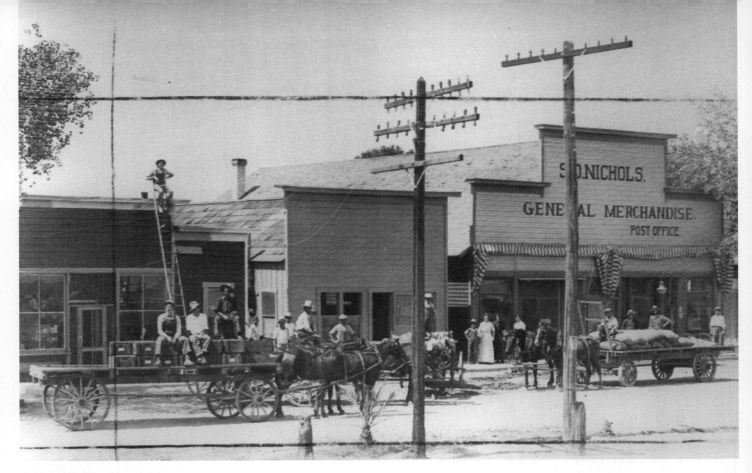

This business block in Thermal was destroyed in a 1915 fire, the first of several fires which ultimately decided the fate of what was once the largest city in the Coachella Valley.

Thermal

The next town, traveling south on the railroad, was Kokell. It had a post office in 1901, the same year that its name was changed to Thermal. By 1910, the Thermal area had become the most rapidly growing area in the valley.

The first school district was formed in 1902, and the first school was built in 1907. The Thermal Baptist Church was built in 1905, the same year as the Fleetwood Hotel, reputed to be the finest hotel in the valley. It became a popular meeting place with an excellent dining room. Lucy Laflin, who came to Thermal to teach school in 1916, recalled many happy times in the parlor of the hotel. Single teachers and the local bachelor farmers joined in sing-a-longs—considered a proper activity by the school board.

J. W. Newman stands on his wagon loaded with date offshoots, in front of the Thermal Town Hall. Newman was a successful farmer, telephone company owner, member of the first Storm Water Board and a director of the Coachella Valley County Water District for sixteen years.

Right: The first school in Thermal served all eight grades. Teachers were expected to attend the Thermal Baptist Church and not to go to Indio on Saturday night.

Thermal's business district included the Town Hall, built in 1908, the *Submarine* newspaper office, a large rooming house which housed grape workers who came down from Fresno for the harvest, a pool hall, a bank, several general stores, and a small cement building which housed the telephone switchboard and its operators. The Triple A Water Company made use of an artesian well which had simply flowed down the road for many years. Water lines were run across the road to the railroad siding so tank cars could be filled with drinking water for Imperial Valley. Water of excellent quality from Thermal area wells is still being sold to bottling companies in the 1990s.

Hitching posts and watering troughs along the streets accommodated the customers who arrived on horseback or in wagons. Runaways were a problem when a passing train "spooked" the horses. The town constable was kept busy on Halloween meeting the challenge of would-be cowboys from the Westside ranches, set upon overturning outhouses and doing other mischief.

A 1919 fire destroyed Hotel Fleetwood and a large portion of the town. The hotel was by far the greatest loss and the newspaper reported, "It was an asset to the valley. . . . It was here we could depend upon having our visiting friends properly taken care of."

The original telephone switchboard, used from 1906 to 1924, was located in Thermal because of its central location between Indio and Mecca. Gilberta Harmon and Mary Ann Bundschuh Trager were two of its early operators. The central office had only two lines into Indio and service was limited to use between 6 AM and 9 PM. Only emergency calls could be made at other times.

This is a Hotel Fleetwood menu.

The Coachella Valley High School had its beginning in the spring of 1910. Indio, Coachella, and Thermal each wanted the school in their community, but none had the proper facilities. It was learned that Indio would have no students that year. Thermal had just built a new four-room grammar school, leaving the "Little Green School House" vacant, so high school opened there with eight students and one instructor, Mr. J. W. Warren. He must have been a wonder, for in *The Date Palm* of March 1911, the editor reported, "Coachella Valley Union High School—not open a year—offers Grammar and Composition, Literature, History, Political Economy, Civics, Latin, Chemistry, Physics, Physical Free Hand Drawing, Physiology, Bookkeeping, General

Hotel Thermal was originally built to house the valley's first high school.

Coachella Valley High School was finally begun on the ten-acre Narbonne property in 1916. Besides the fact that the land was a gift, trustees were gratified that its location isolated young boys from the pool halls of the communities! There were five graduates in 1916.

Local ladies attended a class in Indian basketry at the new high school in 1916.

Agriculture, Botany, and Commercial Arithmetic. Our Boys and Girls can secure a thorough preparation for the University." In 1911 and 1912, attendance increased and an additional instructor was hired and the Thermal Baptist Church furnished additional classroom space. Mabel Lehman Wise reminisced that the small room in the church steeple, where she taught, was very hot and populated by bats—not the best place for learning to take place!

In 1913 the high school trustees approached Mattie Alderman, who had purchased six blocks in Thermal, to build permanent facilities for the school for the next two years. Funds were not available to build on the property on Avenue 56, given to the district by G. H. Narbonne. Mrs. Alderman agreed to borrow money to build a school on her property, assured by a "Gentlemen's Agreement" that the building would be rented by the district for two years. She built a spacious assembly room with a huge fireplace and four classrooms. At the close of the first year, someone anxious to have the school in Coachella moved all of the school materials to Coachella, leaving Mrs. Alderman "holding the bag" for a way to pay off her debt. Arrangements were made to accommodate lodgers and Hotel Thermal was born!

Mrs. Alderman's daughter, Gilberta Harmon, shared her mother's early struggles and continued to live in Hotel Thermal until her death in the 1990s. She became one of the earliest "Chief Operators" of the early telephone company. Company reports indicate there were between 100 and 120 telephones in service between 1906 and 1919. Gilberta trained operators who personally connected every call. Most of the lines were listed as ten-party lines but in reality the number of parties depended on the ingenuity of the operators determining new code rings to identify customers. Sometimes as many as sixteen or eighteen were connected on one line. If a storm caused lines to be down, farmers ran the phone lines from fence post to fence post until a repair crew would determine there was "sufficient work" to justify their going to the area of the downed poles. Interestingly, most of the early telephone poles came as salvage from the railroad telegraph lines inundated by the rise of the Salton Sea.

Thermal had become the agricultural hub of the valley. Farmers' Institutes were held in the Thermal Town Hall and top speakers from the U.S. Department of Agriculture and the University of California came to discuss pertinent issues.

The Date Palm reported that in September 1912 several young men met in Thermal to form a club known as the "Bachelors' Club." The object was "to be promoting association and marketing of produce by ranchers, boosting and promoting all good movements, and also to make their social life more pleasant. Officers were elected, quarters found and furnished, and it was announced that any single male was eligible, the name to be submitted and voted upon. The quarters consisted of three rooms. In the first was a large reading table, comfortable chairs, magazines, books, and stationery. There was also in the room a gramaphone and a fine selection of records. The room was beautifully lighted with a gasoline lamp. The adjoining room was for the house committee. Back of this was a well-lighted room . . . for a billiard and pool table."

The club had the support and backing of many of the prominent men of the valley, including Nelson Dilworth, elected as vice president in 1913.

The town of Thermal never recovered from the fires which repeatedly wiped out its business district and many of its homes. When fire destroyed the old packing house used by the Thermal Cantaloupe Growers Union November 26, 1920, *The Date Palm* reported, "The fire fiend again visited Thermal. . . . Aside from the loss of value there is a fine bit of sentiment involved that touched the hearts of all the old pioneers. It was the first packing house built in the town and recalls the old cantaloupe days when excitement ran high and men were millionaires one day and paupers the next. All of the development of the lower valley can be traced directly to this old packing house."

Thermal boasted its own bakery, with delivery service.

By 1914 many Thermal families had built very comfortable homes like this one owned by the Eberhardt family.

According to *The Date Palm,* the Arabia Mercantile Company carried "well-selected merchandise and staple and fancy groceries."

Arabia

Arabia doesn't show up on 1990s maps of the Coachella Valley, but, before 1903, it was a forty-acre townsite just west of Highway 111 between Avenues 60 and 61 (part of Oasis Date Gardens) billed as the "town of the valley." There was a store, a post office, and the valley's first cotton gin, located on its railroad siding. When the owner moved the gin to Thermal in 1920, it marked the beginning of the end for Arabia.

George Durbrow, who owned and operated the Liverpool Salt Works on the Salton Sea laid out a subdivision in Arabia, complete with streets and lots. Durbrow suffered a double loss in 1905–1906 when his salt works were submerged by the rising Salton Sea, and his investments in San Francisco were wiped out by the earthquake and fire.

Today only a wide paved area west of Highway 111, used by road crews for stockpiling asphalt, marks the spot where the cotton gin once stood and the dreams of "one day the leading center of commerce in the fertile Coachella Valley" died.

The John Leach family lived in this home in Arabia in 1913. Their son George had fun explaining why his birth certificate said he was born in "Arabia."

George, Esther, Alice, and Herbert Leach pose in front of their Arabia home. Note the Arabia Cotton Gin in the background.

Coachella Valley

Mecca

Only one hundred years ago Mecca was the hub where teamsters, prospectors, hard-rock miners, camp cooks, and the like gathered before setting out for the "diggings." In fact, before 1900, Mecca was the center of valley activity. Before the discovery of adequate water for agriculture, the excitement in the Coachella Valley was gold. No men were more in demand than experienced teamsters with their heavy wagons and sturdy horses and mules. Mines had to be supplied, and gold and silver ore had to be brought out to the railroad. It took nine hours of heavy pulling through deep sand to reach Shaver's Well, an important watering point at the upper end of Box Canyon, east of Mecca. Beyond that point, two trails branched off, leading to various mines, most of which could be reached in one or two days.

Colorado River water, pouring into the Salton Sink in 1906, came within a quarter of a mile of the town of Mecca, surrounding this and many other homes.

The Southern Pacific built the Walters siding in 1877. In 1903 the name was changed to Mecca. (Courtesy of Coachella Valley Water District)

There was a good spring alongside the railroad track in Mecca. A hole was dug about ten feet down, and a path led to the standing water. Dale Kiler, a pioneer, stated, "Snakes, lizards, coyotes, cows, dogs, Indians and white men all drank from the well, and no one died."

The Mecca area was known for its artesian wells, and farming began there before 1898, the year that 25 acres of cantaloupes were sold for $5 a crate. In 1899 about 225 acres were planted and sold for the same price. Los Angeles papers began reporting that farmers in the Coachella Valley were becoming wealthy, and there was a great rush to take up government land. Kiler estimated that approximately 1,800 acres of melons were planted in 1900. Temperatures reached 135 degrees in June, and the melons spoiled enroute to market. Most of the farmers went broke. Kiler considered himself lucky. He ended the disastrous season with no

This was Mecca about 1904. At left is the Caravansary, gathering place of prospectors and visitors, and at right is the building known as the Mission Store. (Courtesy of Coachella Valley Water District)

Above: Early Mecca settlers included the E. B. Ames family, shown here with neighbors. Paul Ames is in the foreground. (Courtesy of Paul Ames)

income, but only owing the packing house $3 for seed! Mecca's first school was built in 1902, and, in 1905, Kiler married the young schoolteacher who taught Spanish on Saturday evenings.

Mecca was an important watering stop for the railroad and was the point from which a spur railroad ran south about twelve miles to Salton Station. The New Liverpool Salt Company began operation in 1884 when George Durbrow shipped what he called "white gold" to San Francisco. The vast salt deposits, comprising over one thousand acres of unusually pure rock salt, were considered among the largest in the country.

The New Liverpool Salt Company was one of the county's earliest industries.

This little steam engine was used at the salt works until the operation was inundated. The submerged buildings were visible for years when the water of the newly formed sea was clear.

After the salt was smashed by plows, it was piled in conical mounds and then conveyed by tram railway to the salt works. There, workers ground the salt and sacked and shipped it to various markets. The crop was priced from $6 to $34 per ton. It is doubtful if the company ever worked more than a hundredth of the area. In 1901, a rival concern, the Standard Salt Company, contested the New Liverpool's rights to harvest the salt. Ultimately the two companies worked together, but salt mining was doomed. When the Colorado River poured into the Salton Sink in 1905, it covered the entire operation.

Less than eight years after the historic Wright Brothers flight at Kitty Hawk, Robert Fowler landed an airplane in a field near Mecca! The date was October 24, 1911. Fowler was seeking to win a $50,000 prize offered by William Randolph Hearst to the first aviator to complete a transcontinental flight. Fowler chose a route with suitable low-level mountain passes by following the Southern Pacific railroad. This also insured that he would have water, food, communication, mechanical help, parts, and the encouragement of those traveling by train.

The first landing of an airplane in the valley was at Mecca in 1911. (Courtesy of Ray House)

The *Coachella Valley News* reported "Great crowds rushed to Mecca to see the aeroplane. Fully five hundred people thronged the field. . . . Two short trial flights were made over Salton Sea and the surrounding country. The night was spent there and another trial flight made Wednesday morning. The motor was thoroughly overhauled and at 8:25 AM Mr. Fowler climbed into his seat. He rose to the north and sailed toward the hills. Turning a few times over Mecca and the sea, he was satisfied with his motor and headed to the southeast for Yuma. His speed increased tremendously and soon the flyer was but a speck in the sky."

Fowler ultimately landed at his destination, Jacksonville, Florida, on February 8, 1912—too late to claim Hearst's prize— but he was the first man to cross the continent from west to east. Meanwhile another aviator, Cal Rodgers, made the flight from New York to California and his forty-nine-day flight took him over Mecca also, since he, too, used the "iron compass"—the railroad tracks. He did not land, but the valley turned out to see him soar overhead.

Both men were flying Wright biplanes constructed of wood, wire, and muslin. When Rodger's trip was complete, the only original parts left on his tattered plane were the vertical rudder, the drip pan, and a strut holding a bottle of Vin Fiz, his sponsor's product. *American Heritage* called it "Coast to Coast in Twelve Crashes."

Both the David Foulkes family and the E. B. Ames family arrived in Mecca in 1914. Ames purchased eighty acres from the

Box Canyon, east of Mecca, was a favorite spot for an outing. According to his daughter, Margaret Tyler, Hugh Proctor, and friends were probably enjoying Grand Opera.

Southern Pacific Land Company, pitched a tent, and proceeded to clear the land. Using two mules to pull a homemade scraper and leveler, Ames prepared to plant alfalfa for seed. He developed a process of eliminating weeds from his field and marketing "weed free" alfalfa seed and the operation was profitable. His grandson, Paul, recalls being offered a bounty by his grandfather for finding and removing any weed that might have crept in.

David and Barbara Foulkes first came to Mecca in 1912, dropped in on a dance at Mecca School, liked what they saw in terms of community spirit, and returned from Los Angeles two years later with five of their eight children. They owned and operated Mecca's Mission Store for many years. Daughter Cecelia graduated from Mecca School in 1915 and returned in later years to become one of Mecca's best-loved schoolteachers. Daughter Rosalie married Dr. Clair Johnson, one of the town's most public-spirited citizens.

This 1896 photograph is believed to depict travelers who followed the Bradshaw Trail into the valley.

The Cove Communities

La Quinta, Indian Wells, Palm Desert, Rancho Mirage, and Cathedral City are communities which originally nestled at the base of the Santa Rosa Mountains on the western side of the valley. The view from a distance reveals the geological fact that each is built on an alluvial plain—sand, rocks, and debris from eons of flooding and the wearing down of the western mountains. It was not the best farmland, and most of the wells that were drilled there did not reach into the main valley aquifer. Furthermore, periodic heavy floods were devastating. La Quinta and Indian Wells both have a substantial agricultural history, but the cities came into existence after 1950.

Indian Wells

It's hard to imagine as you drive along beautifully landscaped Highway 111 today that this area was once only mesquite-covered dunes traversed by a dusty wagon road—well-used because it took travelers past one of the best water sources in the desert. It was noted on earliest maps as "Indian Wells."

The original well was destroyed by flooding, but a county well was constructed nearby. After the Arizona gold strikes of the 1860s, prospectors came pouring across the desert and William D. Bradshaw realized there were profits to be made from the operation of a stage line connecting Los Angeles to the gold fields. Bradshaw, with the cooperation of Chief Cabazon, marked all of the watering places from the San Gorgonio Pass to the Colorado River via the Salton Sink. Indian Wells was a convenient one-day journey from Agua Caliente (present-day Palm Springs) and was almost the same distance from the next main well at the north end of what is now the Salton Sea. A member of one of Indian Wells' earliest families, William Cook, remembered when one could see the wheel and hubcap marks of wagons on the rocks at Point Happy, where the road turned south.

William P. Blair is shown about 1909, cultivating melons on his homestead in the approximate area of the golf resort at Indian Wells.

The Blair brothers were early-day well drillers. (Courtesy of Coachella Valley Water District)

Shown here, in 1909, is William Blair's farm, looking south from the dune south of Palm Desert Country Club. Eisenhower Mountain is in the right rear. In 1916 the Whitewater River carved a channel through the ranch.

The *Indio Index* reported in September of 1909 that "Norman 'Happy' Lundbeck, C. A. Chapin, J. C. O'Neal, P. J. Enright, Mitlerman and Mr. Wm Blair were developing in the Indian Wells area." Lundbeck gave his name to the rocky point that bears the name "Point Happy" today. The Point Happy School District was organized in 1916 and its one-room school operated until the district merged with the Indio Elementary School District in July 1929.

Ruth White Peters, daughter of one of the Point Happy School's early teachers, wrote a wonderfully descriptive account of her mother's life as the one teacher of all eight grades. Children gathered in a square wooden structure with a pyramid roof, sitting atop a sand dune surrounded by miles of open desert. Mrs. Peters says, in part, "The student body ranged in age from 6 to 15 years, farm children and farm laborer's children. . . . Point Happy School enjoyed few holidays. With an uninsulated building and only windows and a door to air-condition a schoolroom that often reached 110 degrees inside, it was desirable to finish school as early in May as possible . . . Today winds in the Coachella Valley can be annoying and inconvenient but they bear no resemblance to the vicious sand storms that swept across the desert in the early decades of the twentieth century. Except for the few isolated farms, there was nothing to break the storm's force from Banning to the Salton Sea. Heavily laden with sand, . . . the wind would sweep across the school yard and slam into the school building, rattling its windows and howling like a banshee. . . . A scoop shovel was kept under the front stoop to clear away the sand so that the door could be opened after a weekend storm."

Ben Harmon and his wife were Indian Wells pioneers.

Early residents had to clear away dense mesquite groves. (Courtesy of Coachella Valley Water District)

Caleb Cook displays one of the rattlesnakes for which Indian Wells was famous. (Courtesy of Palm Desert Historical Society)

The drive between her home in Indio and the school took the better part of forty minutes (in 1924) for although the road was paved, it was very narrow. There were no shoulders of any kind and a car was almost sure to flip over if it dropped off the pavement at speeds exceeding twenty miles per hour.

Rattlesnakes were a real danger for children playing near the mesquite-covered dunes, and one of Mrs. White's little girls was fatally bitten while walking home from school. There were no ambulances, no effective antidotes, no telephones, and actually not much anyone could do. The Indian Wells area was noted for its snake population and one of the settlers made a living collecting rattlesnakes and selling them in Los Angeles for their venom.

Farming was the principal business in Indian Wells until the 1950s. "Happy" Lundbeck had a small store just west of the rocky point. *The Date Palm* of April 2, 1926, carried an article captioned, "Indian Wells Saved" which read, "Indio's fire department made the seven mile run to Indian Wells and saved the whole settlement from destruction by a cane-brake fire that was being fanned to a fury by the wind. An automobile was dispatched to Indio for help and the little fire engine was soon on its way. The irrigation pump was running and the ditch was full of water, so firemen only had to drop the suction pipe into the ditch, string a hundred yards of hose and get into action."

The family for whom Cook Street is named came to the valley in 1912. Caleb Cook was a professor at Whittier College and later a partner in a Los Angeles firm that made scientific laboratory equipment for schools. Told by his doctor that he needed to find outdoor work, he decided that the infant date industry looked promising. He purchased relinquishments on government homesteads south of Indio and he filed a desert claim on 160 acres on the northeast corner of what is now Cook Street and Highway 111.

The family lived on the property south of Indio. When he needed to check on the Indian Wells property he would load provisions onto a spring wagon and spend most of the day getting there. After staying overnight, he spent most of the next day getting home. Electricity came into the valley in 1914 and Cook purchased a Model-T Ford and helped support his family by doing electrical installations all over the area.

The date industry was in its infancy prior to World War I. Cook joined with W. L. Paul in forming the Coachella Valley Date Growers Association, with a primary purpose of importing date palm offshoots, principally the Deglet Noor variety, from North Africa. At the time the association was formed, the government had distributed thousands of date seeds for farmers to plant. The result was widely varied fruit of poor quality, creating real marketing problems.

Ultimately the Deglet Noor growers wanted to separate themselves from the seedling and soft-date variety growers and Cook became president and general manager of the California Deglet Noor Association. In the spring of 1927 he met an untimely work-related death—a great loss to the valley—but his sons, Robert and William, continued to be involved in the date industry.

In 1934 the Deglet Noor Date Growers Association became the California Date Growers Association and William Cook became president and general manager, a position he held until 1950. He built an adobe house on his own 20 acres of sand on Deep Canyon Drive north of Fred Waring Drive. Adobe was a preferred building material because its insulating capacity made the warm summer temperatures quite bearable. The Cooks had an unobstructed view of the mountains, and with a full moon and the sound of coyotes in the distance, Mrs. Cook reported that it seemed like a fairyland.

Indian Wells continued to develop as a farming community. James Arkell, of the Beechnut chewing gum company, engaged Caleb Cook to plant land north of Highway 111 and west of Eldorado Boulevard to Deglet Noor palms. A mansion was built on a dune in the middle of the property, entered through a gate marked "La Finca de Esperanza." Arkell's sister, Mrs. Warren, purchased adjoining acreage and planted it to dates also. These two ranches were sold in the 1970s to the group building Desert Horizons Country Club.

Owners across Highway 111 included Farmer Page of Chicago, A. J. Shamblin, Ralph Wescot, Percy Day, and Bert Cavanagh. Included in their lands are the present-day El Dorado and Indian Wells Country Clubs, and the hotel properties bordering Highway 111.

One Indian Wells pioneer who deserves much credit for its development is Herbert L. "Bert" Cavanagh. Following high school graduation in 1921, he came from Los Angeles, intrigued by the newspaper publicity regarding the date industry. He worked on the Cook properties, saved his money, purchased land, and planted dates. His home place is now the location of the Miramonte Hotel, and the tall palms just west of the hotel are what remains of a beautiful planting of Deglet Noor and Medjool palms.

In an interview with Dr. Ralph Pawley, Bert recalled the transition from farming to the city of Indian Wells. He said, "There was no abrupt change. The farmland up against the Santa Rosa Mountains was sold, and the El Dorado Country Club began building there. Soon after that, the Indian Wells Country Club was going in. In the late 1950s when a trailer court was proposed along Highway 111, a property owners' group was formed within the El Dorado Country Club to fight it."

Area ranchers fought it too, and won. Cavanagh continued, "We knew that our time was going to be limited as far as ranching there and if it wasn't going to be used for ranching, we did not want it turning into a shanty town. Resort development seemed the best possible use.

"It was much the same in 1967 when the people of Indian Wells voted to incorporate. Down the road, Palm Desert was preparing to incorporate, absorbing Indian Wells in the process. To the people of Indian Wells, bent on preserving a life-style, the choice was obvious. The reason for incorporation was self-defense. Thus on July 16, 1967, the two country clubs became the city of Indian Wells."

A three-mule team on the Cook ranch provided the power for releveling and building borders with a Fresno Scraper.

Indian Wells has continued to make the transition with the building of the Grand Champions and Renaissance Esmeralda resort hotels on the north side of Highway 111. Its commercial buildings reflect the city's desire to carefully plan its growth. Water, which first brought both Indians and white settlers to Indian Wells, is still plentiful, thanks to the domestic water facilities of the Coachella Valley Water District, and their constuction of stormwater channels which have become a part of the area's golf courses. The main channel of the Whitewater River passes through the community, a broad expanse of sloping green lawn, ready to carry the sudden flow of a desert river.

This is the La Quinta Hotel in 1930.

La Quinta

The lower part of the La Quinta area was once an old lake bed, covered with clay and spotted with sand dunes. It was a good place to find Indian arrowheads and other artifacts—proof of its use by the Cahuilla people. Its clay was supposed to be the best in the valley for making ollas. Dr. Ralph Pawley wrote this about the area that was first called Marshall Cove:

In 1902 John Marshall and his brother-in-law homesteaded 320 acres of land at the south end of Washington Street and Avenue 52. They divided the land into two 160 acre pieces. Albert Green took the 160 acres east of Washington Street and John Marshall took the 160 acres west of Washington. . . . Green sold his land. John Marshall hired a man to clear, level, and plant part of his land. A well was drilled, a house was built, and Marshall furnished the work animals, ranch equipment, wagon, buggy, and a cow.

Farming went well until about 1910 when the hired man disappeared, leaving the ranch animals and chickens unattended. John sent his son from Los Angeles to the ranch to gather up and cook the chickens and return to Los Angeles with three horses, the wagon and cow. It took Harry seven days to travel from the ranch to Los Angeles in the wagon, leading a horse and a cow. The horses and wagon were used in the paint business in which Marshall and Green were involved. . . .

John Marshall decided to divide the paint business with Albert Green, . . . keeping the retail paint store which he turned over to his son, Harry. John then bought a home in Indio, and purchased all the unsold lots in the Indio townsite from Mrs. Gard, as well as the Indio Water System. He bought a Ford and traveled back and forth between his ranch and Indio, doing what he enjoyed most in life—farming.

In 1920 a large hacienda-style house and workers' cottages were constructed. A large swimming pool served as an irrigation reservoir. Citrus was the main crop, but there was also a block of date palms, and the row of stately eucalyptus along what is now "old" Avenue 52. John Marshall died in a well cave-in in 1938, after having made a significant impact on the early development of La Quinta Cove. The lake that formed at the base of the cove, when flash-floods roared down out of the Santa Rosa Mountains, was known as Marshall Lake.

Harry Marshall sold the ranch to William S. Rosecrans, a wealthy Los Angeles oil man, and it was the Rosecrans family that gave the ranch its name, "Hacienda del Gato." According to legend a little grey cat was responsible for saving Mrs. Rosecrans from a large rattlesnake just outside the kitchen door. The cat lived for twenty years after the incident and was buried in a small grave near the swimming pool.

Reputedly Rudolph Valentino was a guest at the ranch in the 1920s and other celebrities are also said to have enjoyed its tranquil setting.

In 1910 Manning Burkett homesteaded 160 acres of land about a mile south of present Highway 111 and east of Washington Street. He had a well drilled, built his own home, leveled the land, and began farming row crops and later citrus.

The Point Happy Ranch, at the corner of present Highway 111 and Washington Street was homesteaded by Norman "Happy" Lundbeck around 1900. It had a stable and small store on the premises and in 1916 a one-room school which was relocated a few years later to land west of the point. The school district boundaries included over 190 square miles and included present-day Palm Desert, Indian Wells and La Quinta, as well as a strip eight miles wide that extended across the Santa Rosa Mountains to the southern county line.

Chauncey and Mary Clark purchased the Point Happy property around 1915 according to Dr. Pawley—1922 by other accounts. They increased the holdings to 135 acres. Wells were drilled, the land cleared and planted with dates and citrus. They hired Manning and Rufford Burkett to build a modern

This early homestead of Manning and Mary Burkett was on Washington Street, across from today's St. Francis of Asissi Church. (Courtesy of the Burkett family)

The adobe bricks in the Burkett house were made from La Quinta clay. (Courtesy of the Burkett family)

California-style home. In addition, they built two swimming pools, tennis courts, an archery course, bridle paths, and beautiful flower gardens.

Clark was interested in breeding horses so corrals, barns, and living quarters for the trainers were built. Clark purchased eleven head of fine Arabian horses, supposed to be descendents of the horse God gave to Ishmael as compensation for being disinherited by his father Abraham. Clark planned on cross-breeding the Arabians with Scotch-hunter horses to produce excellent polo ponies. Visitors from around the world, interested in Arabian horses, visited the ranch. An article in the *Los Angeles Times* of March 8, 1925, states, "Chauncey D. Clarke is a very enthusiastic booster for the dates and horses of the old world desert lands. The desert climate and conditions, he believes, offer the finest training ground for making the horses both sure-footed and strong in shoulders and joints. In other words, he believes that conditions in the Coachella Valley are so similar to those in Arabia, where Arab horses have been developed to perfection, as to afford an ideal environment for the raising of this notable breed of the equine kingdom."

When Mr. Clark died in 1926 his horses went to the Kellogg Ranch in Pomona, where the Cal-Poly Pomona campus was developed in later years. Mrs. Clark was known for her generous support of worthy causes and her gracious hosting of visitors to Point Happy Ranch. During World War II, servicemen from Camp Young and other desert installations enjoyed her swimming pools and gardens. She was a founder of the Hollywood Bowl and the Pilgrimage Play, and she loaned the money needed to build the Indio Women's Clubhouse. She died in 1948.

Point Happy Date Gardens was later sold to Mr. William DuPont Jr. who built a home with a spectacular view in a saddle on the rocky spur that is "Point" Happy, and in the date grove below he built a lovely Spanish home for tennis-great Alice Marble. Under new owners, Point Happy Ranch still functions as an agricultural operation and its rocky contours are a valley landmark.

According to an article in the 1951 Palm Springs Yearbook, the La Quinta Hotel may well be the result of a pact made in a front-line trench during the World War I. Two bitterly cold young officers named Ikes and Morgan resolved that if they lived through the war, they would return to the United States and seek the driest, warmest and most enjoyable climate they could find and settle down.

They found that place in the north end of Marshall Cove. They built homes and planted date trees. Then Morgan, the youngest son of a wealthy San Francisco businessman, decided to build a small secluded retreat. He purchased 1,400 acres in the lower cove of an area the Cahuilla Indians called "Happy Hollow"—a term describing its sheltered warmth. In 1926, Morgan hired C. N. Sinclair of Indio to construct six adobe cottages, an office, and a lobby and dining facilities. The hotel opened in February 1927 and represented a total investment between $150,000 and $200,000.

Mrs. Chauncey Clark loved to entertain at her beautiful *Point Happy Ranch*. (Courtesy of the Burkett family)

The goal of the La Quinta Hotel was to lure the rich and famous to a hideaway where they could attend social functions, or simply relax and enjoy the beauty and peacefulness of their own little "casita." And, the people came. Unfortunately the crash of the stock market in 1929 spelled disaster for the Morgan family. The hotel remained open, but with few customers, it was soon in the hands of receivers. A San Francisco hotel owner, Fredrick Clift leased it in 1931 and Marshall Cove was renamed La Quinta, after the hotel. There are several theories as to the meaning of the name, but the hotel's founder said he chose the name for the hotel to reflect the ambience of a Mexican country home, called "La Quinta."

The hotel closed during World War II because gasoline and tire rationing made travel difficult, but before and after that period Hollywood's brightest stars were patrons. Frank Capra discovered the hotel in 1939 when he and screenwriter Robert Briskin secluded themselves in one of the cottages to write the script for *Lost Horizon*, which starred Ronald Coleman. Coleman and his wife were among celebrities such as Errol Flynn, Dolores Del Rio, Eddie Cantor, Dick Powell, Greta Garbo, and Shirley Temple and family who all enjoyed the La Quinta Hotel. Irving Berlin is said to have written "White Christmas" while staying in one of the little desert cottages. The center of the old hotel still stands, surrounded now by guest wings containing hundreds of rooms and all of the amenities of a first-class resort.

In 1932, Harry Kiener, of the Big Bear Land and Water Company, saw the opportunity to start a major residential development in La Quinta. He purchased several thousand acres of land around the La Quinta Hotel and south into the cove. Original lots were 50 by 100 feet and sold for $500 with $25 down. Kiener built some prototype homes which he sold as "week-end homes," completely furnished including linens, for $2,500. Streets were graded but not paved. He promised homebuyers a recreational club, restaurant, and swimming complex and the Desert Club was built in 1937. Its facilities drew many to the club in the days before any municipal pools. Its "Summer Membership" was a boon to families who had to remain through the heat.

Above: Palm Springs' early development was a credit to Judge McCallum, shown here with his wife and family. (Courtesy of Palm Springs Historical Society)

Rock-lined irrigation ditches brought water nineteen miles to Palm Springs from Whitewater and Snow Creek, and from Tahquitz Creek.

Pictured here is downtown Palm Springs in 1900. (Courtesy of Palm Springs Historical Society)

La Quinta was incorporated in 1982, and has expanded its boundaries out of the cove both to the north and the south. Its new civic center, shopping centers, golf resorts such as PGA West, and development along Washington Street attest to its bright future.

Palm Springs

Envisioning an agricultural center which would ship early produce to Los Angeles, John Guthrie McCallum became the first non-Indian to settle permanently in the oasis known as Agua Caliente. McCallum was a San Francisco lawyer who brought his family to the desert, hoping that the warm, dry climate would help his young son who was suffering from tuberculosis. Local Indians helped him build an adobe home which is still in existence as the headquarters for the Palm Springs Historical Society. On March 25, 1885, he signed a deed purchas-

ing his first property, and over the next eight years he acquired over 6,000 acres.

With partners, McCallum founded the Palm Valley Land and Water Company. Brochures promised "Earliest Fruit Region in the State; Absolute Cure for all Pulmonary and Kindred Diseases; Perfect Climate; Wonderful Scenery." A subdivision called Palmdale was begun on the site of the present Smoke Tree Ranch. Passengers took the Southern Pacific trains to the station at Seven Palms and were transported to a hotel McCallum had convinced Dr. Welwood Murray of Banning to build. Murray leased hot springs from the Indians and built a bath house for his guests' use. The Palm Springs Hotel became the village's first resort.

By the early 1890s there were flourishing orange groves, vineyards, fig plantations, and farms producing alfalfa and vegetable crops. Unfortunately there was a record rainfall in 1893 which washed out miles and miles of irrigation ditches, cutting off the farmers' water. Eleven years of drought followed. By the time the drought ended in 1905, trees and vines were dead, settlers had moved away and McCallum himself had died. His daughter, Pearl, carried her father's dreams of a desert oasis into the twentieth century.

Dr. Welwood Murray acquired the title "Dr." during the Civil War when he cared for the wounded on a warship. He had homes both in Banning and in Palm Springs. (Courtesy of Palm Springs Historical Society)

Meanwhile, Dr. Murray had planted an array of experimental trees around his hotel, making it a showplace. His guests also enjoyed Palm Springs' primary natural feature, its hot springs, and also trips into the palm canyons.

In 1909, Dr. and Mrs. Harry Coffman purchased one of the sanatoriums which had been established to care for the respiratory patients, and they opened Dr. Harry Coffman's Desert Inn and Sanatorium. In 1915 Nellie Coffman dropped the word "Sanatorium" from the name. Her husband had moved to Thermal to start another sanatorium, so she and her sons specified in their advertising "No Invalids." This put their establishment in a different class, and removed the fear of communicable disease from prospective clients' minds. By 1926 the Desert Inn had a worldwide reputation.

Dr. Murray died in 1914 and the White sisters, Cornelia and Florilla, bought his hotel. Both became very influential in the village, for village best describes Palm Springs before 1920. J. Smeaton Chase, in his delightful little book, *Our Araby*, published in 1920, writes, " 'Village' is a pretty word, though ambitious settlements are keen to disclaim the implied rusticity and to graduate into the rank of town or city. Palm Springs has no such aims. . . . We decline to take part in the race for Improvements, and are (so we feel, anyway) wise enough to know when we are well off. Rural Free Delivery does not entice us; we prefer the daily gathering at the store at mail-time, Indians and whites together. . . . Electric lights? No, thanks; somehow nothing seems to us so homelike for the dinner-table as shaded candles, or for fireside reading a good kerosene lamp; while if we want to call on a neighbor after dark, we find that a lantern sheds light where you need it instead of illuminating mainly the upper air. To us cement sidewalks would be a calamity."

The Palm Springs Hotel welcomed potential settlers as well as vacationers. Dr. Murray turned the grounds into a botanical garden. (Courtesy of Palm Springs Historical Society)

In 1898 the Palm Springs Hotel offered its patrons a shady spot for a card game and a few beers. (Courtesy of Palm Springs Historical Society)

John Muir, visiting Palm Springs in 1905 when the temperature reached 110 degrees, found the shade inviting at Dr. Murray's hotel. (Courtesy of Palm Springs Historical Society)

Chase continues in praise of the kind of people who appreciate the natural beauty and ambience of Palm Springs. He estimated that there might be a population of 200 in the winter and spring, but no more than a dozen or two in the summer. But Palm Springs was already playing host to the rich and famous, including several who were writers and artists, capable of spreading the word about its charms. And, probably most influential in terms of future growth was the embryonic movie industry. Palm Springs became the locale for stories set in such places as Arabia, North Africa, and Mexico. Its proximity to Los Angeles, its exotic scenery, and its popularity with early screen stars made Palm Springs a household word then, as now.

Nellie Coffman, who arrived in 1908, influenced the direction of Palm Springs' growth for many years. Her son, Earl, was one of the prime movers and first president of the Palm Springs Aerial Tramway Authority. (Courtesy of Palm Springs Historical Society)

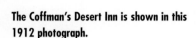

The Coffman's Desert Inn is shown in this 1912 photograph.

Desert Inn Grounds, Palm Springs, California.

Dining room and lobby, The Desert Inn,
Palm Springs, California.

Part III–The Valley After 1920

By 1924 there was regular bus service into the valley.

The 1920s

Health care services, roads, controlling floodwaters, and replenishing the underground water supply were four areas of concern which are dealt with in separate chapters of this book. Building on the work of the first settlers, people in the 1920s set about refining life.

Chapter Seven

Clubwoman Dr. June Robertson McCarroll, eighth from left, in white dress, is credited with having the idea for, and accomplishing the acceptance of, the white center line we take for granted today on our highways.

This picture of the road from Indio to Edom dramatizes the far-reaching effects of the "center line" idea.

This 1924 view of the narrow paved highway, with a "soft shoulder" demonstrates the need for a "center line."

Dr. June Robertson McCarroll, the valley's first resident doctor had retired. Her practice had taken her from Palm Springs to the Salton Sea. Traveling as she did, she had more than a few experiences of being forced off a newly paved highway by drivers that could not tell where their half of the road lay. One day, on the road to Kane Springs, she noticed that the road had been widened from eight feet to sixteen feet, creating a ridge down the center. "That's it," she cried. "We need a line down the center of our highways." Records show that she took her idea to the Board of Supervisors, the Highway Department, and local Chambers of Commerce for seven years, without success. She even paid a man to paint a white line down a one-mile stretch of present Highway 86, past her home in Coachella. Finally, acceeding to the persistence of the county, district, and State Federation of Women's Clubs, in November of 1924, the Highway Commission decided to give the idea a trial. Soon mile after mile of white lines were leading California and America's motoring millions to greater highway safety—all brought about because of the persistence of one country doctor turned clubwoman!

Dr. S. S. M. Jennings was one of Doc June's replacements. He settled on a farm south of Thermal, intending to be primarily a date grower. He soon found himself making house calls all over the valley and in doing so, he realized the water level in wells was dropping alarmingly. His sense of responsibility led him to become not only the valley's beloved physician but one of the chief organizers of the Coachella Valley Water District. He served as president of the first board elected in 1918 until his resignation in 1928.

The 1920s saw date grower organizations formed, packing houses built, and date gardens planted from Palm Springs to the Salton Sea. The DaVall family of Rancho Mirage developed a promising seedling tree into a date they called "Honey."

In 1927, the same Dr. Swingle who made some of the first importations of offshoots returned to Morocco, hoping to get offshoots of a large, choice date, known as the Medjool. There were really three problems—sheiks did not want to sell their offshoots, there was a war going on between the Berbers and the French, and a very serious plant disease was killing the Medjool trees. Nevertheless, Swingle managed to find a remote oasis, called Bou Denib, where the trees seemed to be disease-free. Waiting for the French Foreign Legion to catch up with him to provide protection for his trip, he made friends with the local sheik and got permission to buy eleven offshoots. They were packed in a large box at the army post and shipped at once to the United States.

Plant Quarantine authorities demanded that the offshoots be grown under strict quarantine in a state in which there were no date palms. The extreme southern tip of Nevada seemed to have the right climate, and an amazing survival story ensued. Frank Thackery of the USDA station in Indio picked up the rather dry offshoots at the railroad station in Needles. In 116-degree heat he drove to a run-down farm belonging to an elderly Chemehuevi Indian couple named Johnson. He secured a promise from them to care for the eleven offshoots, and he promptly planted all eleven. Looking for some cool earth, dogs dug up two offshoots which Johnson burned, but the remaining nine survived. They were kept in isolation for more than seven years while repeated inspections found no signs of disease or insect pests. It was finally decided to transplant them to the government gardens in Indio in the summer of 1935. In addition to the original nine, there were sixty-four new offshoots which had grown up around them. Under the expert care of George Leach, every one survived and they were eventually distributed to local date growers. The Bayoud disease virtually wiped out the Medjool as a commercial date in Morocco, but offshoots from the transplants to California have been used to plant hundred of acres of Medjools here and all over the world.

Photographs tell some of the highlights of the 1920s.

Valley Independent Bank is the successor to First National Bank of Coachella which moved into this handsome building in Coachella in 1920. Harry Westerfield and his brother, John, established the bank in 1912, making it the oldest continuously operating banking institution in the valley.

Right: Harry Westerfield managed to steer his bank through the Crash of 1929, while active in civic and church affairs.

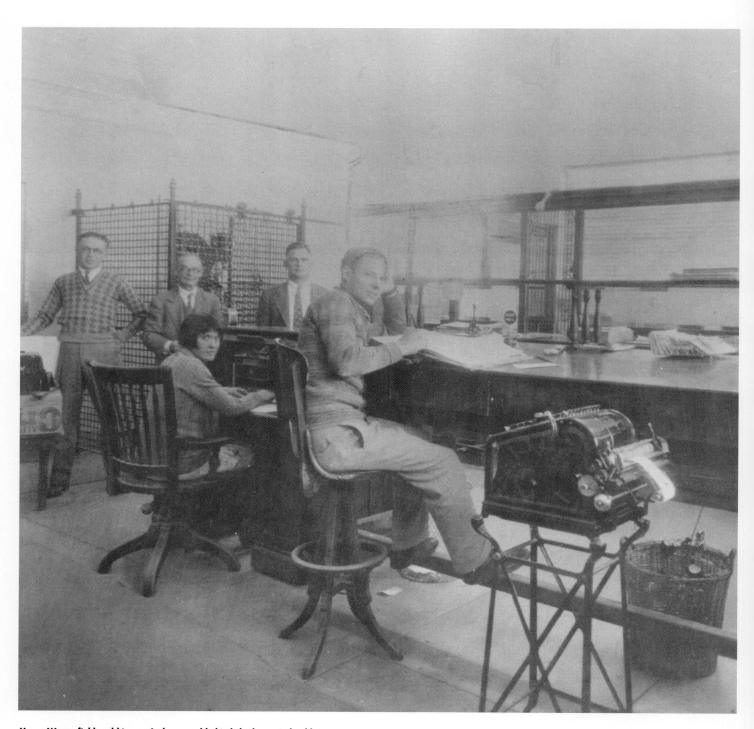

Harry Westerfield and his son Arthur stand behind the latest in bookkeeping equipment.

Arthur and John Westerfield, shown in this 1950 photograph, succeeded their father in heading the First National Bank of Coachella.

Indio's first fire truck was purchased in 1924.

Orville Maynard, Ray Thomas, Gene Runyon, and Stanley Allen were proud of Indio's first airport in 1927.

Lucy Smythe sold all sorts of knicknacks downstairs in her "Hopi House" store in downtown Coachella. Constructed in 1926, it became sort of a museum, for she collected old items used by the early settlers, and items people brought in to trade for her regular merchandise. She ordered Navajo rugs from the reservation in Arizona and was reported to have grubstaked many prospectors even though she never realized a dime from any of their ventures. She had a story for every one of the Indian baskets in her priceless collection.

This 1920s view of the Deglet Noor Date Growers packing house and crew illustrates the organization that had occurred in the date industry.

Inside the packing house, workers handled the fruit, supervised by Leonhardt Swingle, brother of the man who imported many offshoots.

Grading the dates by hand insured that Coachella Valley dates were the finest on the market.

This view of a Coachella Valley date garden bears out the belief that the symetry of a mature date grove probably inspired the columns of the earliest temples built in Egypt and the Middle East.

Lee and Ruth Anderson typified the post–World War I couples who began growing dates in the 1920s. Daughters Cathy and Charlotte helped with the sweet potato harvest which paid the bills while they waited for the young date trees to produce the fruit that made Covalda Date Company famous. (Courtesy of the Anderson family)

Lucille Tune Cavanaugh and Joyce Pearson Reddish were Indio's twin ambassadors, dispensing smiles and local dates to customers at "Mac" McCausland's Richfield station. McCausland was chief of the Indio Volunteer Fire Department which in 1934 was called "the best volunteer fire department in the state" by the Board of Fire Underwriters.

The 1930s

Coachella Valley played a key role in an amazing undertaking—a plan to bring Colorado River water to the thirsty coastal plain of Southern California. Without supplementary water, the Los Angeles Basin and Orange County could never have grown into what they are today.

With the completion of the transcontinental railroad there was a tide of incoming settlers, lured to the West by reports of the mild climate and good soil. Underground water supplies, however, soon proved inadequate. The Owens River was tapped, but the search continued for other sources. Getting a share of Colorado River water seemed the most logical next step. On December 28, 1928, thirteen directors of the newly authorized Metropolitan Water District (MWD) met to form a district that included eleven cities, was 624 square miles in area, and contained at that time a population of 1,600,000. Moving Colorado River water required more than just building an aqueduct. Preliminary steps included the authorization by Congress of the construction of Boulder Dam to generate the power needed to pump water through the aqueduct. Parker Dam, 155 miles downstream, also was needed to regulate the flow of the river below Boulder Dam and to provide a storage basin for the aqueduct intake.

What made this undertaking unique was that all costs of the aqueduct were paid for by those living within the district. A $200,000,000 bond issue paid for the construction, with actual costs coming in at $20,000,000 under the original estimates. They got a terrific "buy," which included:

92 miles of 16 feet in diameter tunnels,
63 miles of concrete-lined canals,
55 miles of concrete conduit 16 feet in diameter,
29 miles of inverted siphons,
 3 dams and 5 pumping stations,
237 miles of high-voltage lines from Boulder Dam to power the pumping stations
215 miles of water distribution lines.

The chosen route came west from Parker Dam to the mountains east of Indio, turned slightly north and west and tunneled through the mountains that line the eastern side of the Coachella Valley, then crossed under the Whitewater River and tunneled through Mt. San Jacinto to reach the Riverside plain. The Parker route had been chosen, not because it was the most economical to build but because it required less power to pump water through the line, and it involved fewer miles paralleling the San Andreas fault. It was the largest construction project in the world at the time.

Precast pipe sections were delivered to Indio by railroad flatcar.

This is payday for some of the men lucky enough to have a job during the Depression. To be eligible to work on the Metropolitan Aqueduct they were supposed to be residents of one of the MWDs member cities, but there were always ways to get around the rule. A flophouse on San Julian Street in Los Angeles became famous as home to 2,000 registered residents. A $5 payment to the owner guaranteed a "yes" to the question of residency!

On Christmas Eve 1932, a gang of men left Los Angeles to build the first construction camp at Fargo Canyon, east of Indio. The Depression was on and a job was the best Christmas gift anyone could receive. It was a gift to the Coachella Valley, and especially to Indio and Coachella. Merchants outdid themselves trying to get business from the construction camps. Some 1933 newspapers reported that Indio hotels had installed cooling systems, and restaurants were staying open for aqueduct clientele during the summer. In a related article, it was reported that over two hundred miles of steel water pipe had arrived at the three stations of Garnet, Indio, and Mecca.

In 1934, Indio proclaimed "Aqueduct Miners' Day" and advertising made it the talk of the state. A key event was the Hard-Rock Drilling Contest. The paper stated, "Thirty-five teams of valiant men, each team consisting of a driller and a chuck-tender, have been entered so far from the various camps along the aqueduct. Nothing of the kind, on such a scale, has ever been staged before in the history of the world. People who never saw an air drill in operation are interested and they are coming by hundreds and thousands. The hotels of Indio, La Quinta and Palm Springs are already full and many of the overflow have found quarters in Banning." The affair was a huge success. The team from Wide Canyon Tunnel was the winner of the $500 first prize. Indio's merchants clearly had produced a winning community event.

In 1935 the aqueduct project was ready for steel, and a huge order was placed with the steel works in Youngstown, Ohio. The MWD would need the equivalent of the nation's entire production for five months. A front-page article in the Youngstown paper stated that the order for steel pipe sent to Indio helped take 8,000 people off the Youngstown charity rolls in June.

Contracts for the various parts of the project were given to different construction companies, and many worked simultaneously to complete their share of the work. The miner's biggest fight was with Mt. San Jacinto, the 10,831-foot mountain barrier between the desert and the Los Angeles Basin. The struggle lasted six and a half years and was marked by a horrendous problem of flooded tunnels. The tunnel had to be completely sealed so that no water could seep into the tunnel when it began carrying its Colorado River water. There had been protests from farmers and nearby cities that the flow into the tunnels during construction had lowered the water table in adjoining lands, but that was probably untrue.

Work on the aqueduct was ceremoniously concluded, complete with a nationwide radio broadcast of the festivities, as the final concrete was poured at the West Portal of the San Jacinto Tunnel on October 14, 1939. A vast distribution system was completed years later.

Indio can be proud of the part it played in this great construction project. Incorporated in 1930, it managed to maintain law and order with a police force that only numbered three men. The City Council worked closely with the construction companies to provide recreation for aqueduct workers with minimal interference with the normal life of the town. Card rooms were added, restaurants geared up for the hundreds of men who descended on the town each weekend, and there was even a "red-light" district, operated under rules laid down by the Police Department. The only difficulties that arose were caused by men who had overindulged in liquor and become quarrelsome or too boisterous. These fellows were confined in the combined city/county jail to sober up. On Monday mornings, after payday weekends, a bus from the aqueduct contractor would come to the jail early to pick up the culprits and haul them back to the various camps.

Thomas J. Mullan, manager of the Bank of America in Indio for many years, recalled coming to work in 1934 when the branch was handling aqueduct payrolls. They would open on Sundays and holidays to accommodate aqueduct payroll check cashing.

The building of the Metropolitan Aqueduct was not the only Coachella Valley news during the 1930s. On June 29, 1934, the newspaper announced "Contracts Let for Construction of First 32 Miles of All-American Canal." Irrigation water from the Colorado River would ultimately be delivered first to the Imperial Valley and then to the Coachella Valley. A later article announced "Coachella's Separate Contract is Approved by Secretary Ickes." This followed years of effort to avoid becoming a part of the Imperial Valley contract, thereby having to assume a share of the Imperial Valley's considerable indebtedness. It was front-page news in August 1934 when Al Capone's train went through Indio en route from Atlanta to Alcatraz. A. P. Giannini, founder of the Bank of America, visited Indio in 1936 and declared that the depression was over and he envisioned the Coachella Valley as a coming community. He expected Indio to be a city of 10,000 population by the end of 1938.

Flying clubs were organized in the valley. Sig Varian was one of the prime movers in early aviation history here. He would fly his "Jenny" down from Riverside, land in what is now Palm Desert, near his friend, Ray Thomas' property, or perhaps the two would fly on to Thermal and land, as he put

The Jackhammer gained national fame as hard-rock miners swarmed into Indio for fun. It was built in the style of Early West saloons, with a long bar, a dance floor, booths lining the walls, and a mezzanine opening onto the main floor. There were regular floor shows which might include anything from an educated horse to a balloon dancer whose adornment was the favorite target of the enthusiastic crowd—remarkably accurate in deflating the balloons.

Sig Varian and Ray Thomas pose beside their plane at Indio's first airport.

William Kersteiner, on left, who managed the *Cochran/Odlum Ranch*, and Floyd Odlum, on right, are shown as the latter prepared to fly back to his New York offices. He managed his far-flung financial empire from offices on both the west and east coasts, and the southwest decor which he loved was evident in both offices.

it, "in the brush near Sandy Corner." Another favorite landing spot was the dry lake bed in La Quinta, between Eisenhower Drive and Washington Street.

Indio's first airfield was between Highway 111 and Van Buren Street, north of Avenue 48. Part of the land belonged to the Cabazon Indians, but Harry, Alex, and Rafael Jim were good friends of most of the members of the "Aero Club" and they approved of the land use. The Lions Club became interested in the project and persuaded Southern Sierra Power Company to move a powerline which divided the field and created a dangerous situation. The enlarged field was renamed the Coachella Valley Airport when it opened February 22, 1930. American Airlines built an office to house their radio short wave transmitter and receiver, and they also moved a large lighthouse beacon near the building. Two immense floodlights swept the entire field and there were rows of red and blue lights to define the sides of the landing strip. In 1932 American Airlines developed their own emergency landing field about three miles northeast of Indio, and San Gorgonio Pass and Shaver's Summit were marked with beacons for night flying.

The 1930s saw the arrival of two of Coachella Valley's most prominent citizens, Jacqueline Cochran and her husband, Floyd Odlum. *The Date Palm* reported in July 1936, "Airplane Accident Interests Valley." The paper went on to say that Miss Cochran had been forced to land her plane, while speeding at one hundred miles an hour, at the Indianapolis municipal airport because of a fire in the oil line.

This certificate, awarded to Floyd Odlum was in recognition of his support of the U.S. war effort and particularly of his backing of the development of the Atlas missle. Colleagues said, "This brilliant man leapfrogged into the space age and risked his own money to help the U.S. achieve leadership in space exploration."

The story continued, "Two years ago Miss Cochran purchased a tract of unimproved land about three miles south of Indio and has since had much of the land leveled and set out to grapefruit and dates. The most noticeable improvements she has made are two large modern residences of the ultra-Spanish type, representing an expenditure of more than $25,000. Miss Cochran has spent considerable time here during the last winter, traveling

Jacqueline Cochran organized and directed the Women's Airforce Service Pilots, known as WASPS, leading one thousand women pilots who flew warplanes across the Atlantic and on other missions at home. Female pilots were deactivated late in 1944, but Cochran continued to serve as a special consultant to the Army Air Force.

almost exclusively by airplane, of which she owns several, including a large transport plane with a passenger capacity of sixteen. Miss Cochran often brings parties of her friends here from New York and other centers on the Atlantic Coast, giving them an

opportunity to enjoy the Coachella Valley winter climate which she considers the most perfect in this country or elsewhere."

Pioneer aviatrix, Jacqueline Cochran, the penniless orphan who became a successful cosmetics manufacturer and the first woman to fly faster than the speed of sound, was a Coachella Valley resident for nearly half a century. In 1932, four years before she married her famous husband, Floyd Odlum, he suggested that she learn to fly to cover her cosmetics territory. She amazed her

Amelia Earhart is shown with Jackie Cochran as the two shared flying experiences prior to Earhart's 1937 flight which ended with her disappearance in the South Pacific. Jackie always said, "She just fell into the drink."

Colonel Chuck Yeager, first pilot to break the sound barrier, encouraged Jackie to be the first woman to do so. She was successful—just one of her many firsts.

Honors continued to be bestowed on this accomplished flier. In 1963 she set course records in this Lockheed F104G Super Starfighter. She was awarded the Distinguished Flying Cross, the Legion of Merit and in 1971 she was named Honorary Fellow of the Society of Experimental Test Pilots and enshrined in the Aviation Hall of Fame in Dayton, Ohio.

Dr. Edward Teller, one of many influential guests to visit the *Cochran/Odlum Ranch*, is shown here with Jackie Cochran at a birthday party honoring her husband in 1960. President Eisenhower wrote a portion of his memoirs in one of the ranch cottages.

instructor when she earned her license in less than three weeks, launching a career which would make her one of the century's most famous fliers.

The Cochran/Odlum duo entertained the rich and famous at their desert ranch. The nine-hole golf course which they built for their guests in 1947 was the second built in the Coachella Valley. It became an eighteen-hole course in 1974. The ranch was by then Indian Palms Country Club. Helen Dettweiler was the first pro at the course.

This view shows a portion of the Cochran/Odlum home after it became Indian Palms Country Club.

Merle C. Taylor

F.B. Dozier

Art M. Westerfield

Eugene Jarvis

Clair S. Johnson

Fred H. Paine

Delano G

W.D. Dickey

Leonhart Swingle

S.C. McPheeters

Ralph Wool

Ralph Roblee

George Berry

Rufus Choate

A.J. Shamblin

J.W. Newman

Curtis Newman

E. Keith Fo

Jack Walker

Gail Brumwell

J.C. Tyler

Don Mitchell

Harold Taylor

P.B. Churchman

Earl B

Winn G. Jenkins

W.W. Cook

Frank Freeland

Harry H. Moore

R. MacKenzie

Perry Van Der Meid

Clarence

ard Hayward   Fred Woolpert   Jim G. Nusbaum   Lon Harvey

lace Rouse   Leonard Rygg   G.L. Ritchey   Joe E. MacDonald

. Dykes   Roy W. Nixon   Howard S. Carr   Fred Becker

nley Hayward   John N. Vevers   Ralph Groves   Frank Masters

R. Pratt   Hugh W. Proctor   Frank A. Thackery   John M. Kelley

Indio was ready for the Western Days parade in 1939.

Right: Western Days brought out the whiskers and Old West garb on Wallace Rouse, A. Rolland, Frank Purcell, Frank Tebo, C. A. Washburn, and Hugh Moore.

The Indio Women's Club parade entrants included Dr. June McCarroll (with parasol).

Zane Grey's *Flying Sphynx Ranch* entered this float in the 1939 parade. The Oasis-area ranch was managed by Walter Pulsifer.

Left: This vintage photograph of the Bank of America staff, circa 1939–1940 includes, in the back row, Harold Taylor, branch manager, Tom Mullan, assistant manager, and Jackie Cochran, customer. Mullan's career with the bank spanned forty-eight years.

The first home of Our Lady of Perpetual Help Catholic Church was built in Indio in 1937.

Officers participating in a ceremony at Camp Young in 1942 included General Patton, Colonels Pickering, Busch, and Muller, and Captain Copeland.

The 1940s

The Coachella Valley was forever changed as it accepted the challenges of World War II. Military strategists had decided that combat troops would be needed in North Africa. Training in desert warfare was essential, and Major General George S. Patton had already convinced his superiors that tanks were the secret to success there. A 162,000-square-mile area east of Indio was chosen for a training area because of its varied desert terrain, the availability of water from the Metropolitan Aqueduct which flowed under it, the availability of electricity from the Hayfield pumping station, and the proximity of the Southern Pacific railheads in Indio and Coachella as supply depots. Its headquarters, Camp Young, received its first eight thousand trainees in the spring of 1942.

Besides that huge installation, as the war progressed, the Army purchased the El Mirador Hotel in Palm Springs, converting it into Torney General Hospital, primarily for the care of wounded from the South Pacific. They took over Palm Springs Airport as a facility for supply and troop aircraft manufactured near Los Angeles. Barracks lined Tahquitz Way. Camp Young's Motor Pool was stationed in what is now Palm Desert, on a site across from the present George Washington Elementary School. The Thermal Army Air Base was established as a backup facility to March Field in Riverside. About twenty-five thousand troops at a time were trained at Camp Young and 10 percent (2,500) were given passes each afternoon and evening. The men on a particular pass were able to repeat their visit again in ten days. Needless to say, townspeople felt a bit crowded when the sidewalks filled with servicemen and a seat in a cafe or at the movies was not to be had.

The diplomacy of General Patton apparently took care of one complaint. The story is told that the ladies of the Indio Women's Club complained the soldiers whistled at them. General Patton offered to discuss the problem. He told the ladies that the men were used to many restrictions, and if he told them not to whistle, they would stop. However, he allowed as how, if he were the ladies, he would be more concerned if they didn't whistle than

Camp Young tanks covered Palm Desert sand at a site on present Portola Avenue. (Courtesy of Palm Desert Historical Society)

Coachella Valley volunteers watched the skies.

Covalda Date Company, shown in this 1940 photograph, served as a "railhead" for General Patton's supplies. (Courtesy of the Anderson family)

if they did. The ladies agreed, and the men were spared one more "restriction!"

Paydays for the Desert Training Center were a headache. Army finance officers requested money through the Indio Bank of America and the First National Bank of Coachella. Harold Taylor, manager of Bank of America, recalled that the money arrived by registered mail. Military personnel would meet Mr. Taylor at the railroad station with armed military vehicles, receive the money, and take it to the post office. The money was signed over to Mr. Taylor and it was then moved to the bank. The payroll ran two to three million dollars a month and came in bags two feet square and three feet high. Each bag was taken into the vault, opened and counted out for distribution. Guards were stationed on all surrounding streets. The army would run a half-track up to the door and load the payroll, then take off with six soldiers with submachine guns on either side of the truck, convoying out to Camp Young, with an airplane escort overhead.

Indio had grown from a railroad and farming town in the 1920s to a construction boom town in the 1930s. In the 1940s it was handed an invasion. The townspeople responded with warm hospitality, and businessmen counted it their good fortune to have so many customers. Typical of the busy shops was Shepard Jewelry Store on Fargo Street. Lorraine Shepard hired ten wives of army men living in and around Indio as extra clerks. Each night at least one hundred leather wrist bands were sold and the same number of leather caps or "night guards" to slip over the watch during blackouts. Not only the heat but good honest sweat ruined wrist bands in less than two weeks. Like many other valley residents with extra rooms in their homes, the Shepard family housed and gave kitchen privileges to an army family.

A war bride, Betty Graham Bailey, wrote her recollections of Indio in a 1942 letter to the Coachella Valley Historical Society.

Among her memories was swimming in the "lovely pool" at the La Quinta Desert Club—closed for the summer, but opened by the caretaker to officers' wives who drove out nearly every day for a welcome swim.

Bernice Rolland, operator of Rolland's Drug Store, opened her home to every rank of army personnel, many times entertaining General Patton and his wife. Many former soldiers returned at war's end to make the Coachella Valley their home.

An interesting sidelight on the situation at Coachella was related by Cathy Kerby, whose parents, Lee and Ruth Anderson, owned the Covalda Date Packing House. General Patton himself sought them out and asked permission to use their facility as a "railhead"—a shipping depot for supplies. Movement was by truck, but it was still designated a "railhead." After Camp Young got going, Covalda was no longer a supply depot, but it was used for storing and sorting medical supplies. When General Patton came to tell the Andersons "goodbye," junior officers hustled around first, making sure everything was in order, knowing that Patton was a stickler for neatness. They even straightened up the Anderson's office, closing a locking file drawer for which the key had been lost. It was a farewell the Andersons did not soon forget!

Coachella's popular Trading Post became a USO and there were two USOs in Indio. Coachella Valley women gathered to bake doughnuts and roll bandages for the Red Cross, and they, with their husbands, manned the observation towers which searched the skies for enemy planes. One tower still stands at the corner of Airport Boulevard and Highway 111 in Thermal.

Valley farmers saw the introduction of a new crop, guayule. Harry Oliver actually came to the desert to supervise an experimental planting on what was the old Bell ranch, along Highway 99 north of Indio. Harry wrote that "guayule, a native plant of Mexico, produces a messy substance that acts like rubber, except when you want it to, and then it collapses." Harry wrote about the short-lived project with fondness, in his famous "Desert Rat Scrapbook."

The Los Angeles Times of October 12, 1942, carried a front-page article by Staff Writer Ed Ainsworth, who owned a home near the Salton Sea. His love of the desert, and of a very special moment is evident in these exerpts from his story:

"SOLDIERS HEAR SHOSTAKOVICH
California Desert Rings With Martial Music
of Russian Composer"
By Ed Ainsworth

CAMP YOUNG (Near Indio) Oct. 11(Exclusive)
Some terrific musical masterpieces have a prologue. This is the epilogue of Shostakovich. It happened here last night in the desert. Nobody knew what it was going to be like until after it had taken place. It was the mixing of ingredients that never had been blended before—the transplanting of a whole symphony orchestra in dress suits to the middle of a vast wasteland for the benefit of packed thousands of sunbitten young soldiers standing under the glittering stars to hear war music that had been plucked out of the din of battle by another young soldier in the siege of Leningrad.

WAR SYMPHONY
'The Seventh,' or 'War Symphony,' of Dmitri Shostakovich had been presented conventionally in western premiere the night before in Los Angeles. There it was a success. Here it was an epic. On almost limitless sand that a few months before had been scorched wilderness a symphony stage sprang up almost like a mirage. . . . Kleig lights were reflecting against skies that never had known any strange illumination except the burst of a meteor. The few remaining tall, reed-like ocotillos were highlighted as if they were some sort of supernatural batons swaying to direct the almost inaudible melody of the night breeze. Underfoot, the sand was scourged into a thousand criss-cross patterns where

The Trading Post became a popular USO. (Courtesy of Paul Ames)

Palm Springs Airport was taken over for military use during the war. This Western Air Lines plane is shown parked just off the runway in 1940. (Courtesy of the Burkett family)

the lumbering tanks and other armored monsters of war had crawled forward under the blazing sun in simulation of actual desert conflict.

Out in front of the stage, back, back as far as the eye could see and then even farther into the shadows stood the young men, shoulder to shoulder, thousands upon thousands, their faces all turned toward one spot.

DRESS TIES AND SAND
Back of the stage the Los Angeles Symphony Orchestra in tents and in the open calmly got into their dress ties and black jackets . . .

Things started then. Lt. David Bramson called Director Leopold Stokowski to the podium. Then who should stride out to the microphone but 'Little Caesar,' Edward G. Robinson, who started out, 'Listen, youse mugs, pipe down for the big doings.'

He told how Shostakovich, a soldier-composer, only 37, kept leaving his piano to fight fires in Leningrad, burning his hands and burning his soul deeper with the horror and grandeur and glory of it all, and how 'The Seventh' came out of that travail.

Stokowski raised his hands and Shostakovich took over the California desert.

It was universal war music, the language of a warrior overleaping race and language and boundaries. It spoke of the unconquerable fighting heart of the Russian people and the shock of shells and the searing of fire and the slow agony of death and the spirit of ultimate victory . . . The lights shone on the packed masses standing there listening to the martial summons that so many will answer soon as they join the battle at the front. . . . Although the soldier audience had been standing for hours, this dedicatory show of the Camp Young coliseum went on. Jane Winterly, Victor Borge, Ann Miller, Hoagy Carmichael and others performed, free for the soldiers. . . . The orchestra members of Local 47 and all of the entertainers made the 290-mile round-trip by bus or car at their own expense."

The Desert Training Center closed April 30, 1944. Its job was done. The General Patton Museum at Desert Center keeps the memory alive for todays visitors.

There were other interesting sidelights to the war years in the Coachella Valley. Resorts around the Salton Sea became favorite R & R locations for servicemen. A daughter of the owners of Date Palm Beach Resort, June Eilers Hall, met her future husband when he was one of the nearly five hundred men a day who came down from Camp Young. General Patton himself often visited the resort. The Eilers were surprised one day to have a big PBY circle, land, and taxi to the end of their pier. In a short time this was also considered a "Navy Base." When a plane seemed to be heading their way, Mrs. Eilers and daughter June would put a coffee cake in the oven and brew a pot of coffee and by the time the flying boat was anchored, the refreshments were ready for the crew. Mrs. Eilers loyally used Coachella Valley products—grapefruit juice squeezed to order, date bread with salads, and date torte for dessert.

Little was written about it at the time, probably for security reasons, but there was a Navy base on the southwest shores of Salton Sea. In September 1946, the base was taken over by the Sandia Corporation and operated for the Atomic Energy Commission. The sea was used primarily as a bombing range for non-explosive ballistic tests. A valley resident, who lived and worked at Salton Sea Base, said that the optical equipment used there was some of that captured from the Germans in the closing days of World War II—extremely accurate Askania cameras—and

The Salton Sea was a popular recreation spot during the 1940s. (Courtesy of Coachella Valley Water District)

also high speed 35mm Mitchells. These, and other special purpose cameras enabled ground observers to record events of very fast action—too fast for the human eye. It was reported that space

The site of the calcite mine that furnished the crystals needed to build the Norden bombsite is marked by this sign and a jeep road in Anza Borrego State Park.

Harry Oliver, left, and John Hilton, artist and one of the owners of the calcite mine, admire one of John's mineral specimens in his rock shop across from Valerie Jean's date shop. (Courtesy of Paul Ames)

capsule parachutes, drone airplanes and Nike missles were tested at the Salton Sea base until the rising sea in the 1950s caused its abandonment.

This area made at least one other major contribution to the war effort. A secret mine in the mountains west of the Salton Sea contained the only available source of a particular calcite crystal needed to make the Norden bombsight. This transparent crystal formation is sometimes known as Iceland Spar because it is found in cavities in the solidified lava of Iceland. The war in Europe had made shipping in the North Atlantic very precarious and the United States needed another source of this precious commodity. The Norden bombsight was the most accurate in the world and it made possible the success of U.S. bombers in World War II. It was one of the most important U.S. military secrets of the war and was so advanced that bombadiers had to take an oath to protect its secrecy with their lives. Locals who worked the mine remember that it was guarded by Marines and worked around the clock. The

Valerie Jean's, a landmark on Highway 99, was one of many date shops that offered the valley's unique fruit to travelers.

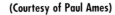

(Courtesy of Paul Ames)

The 1940s

abandoned mine is now within the boundaries of Anza Borrego State Park.

Recycled World War II barracks buildings are still recognizable in many of the valley's communities.

The 1940s are to be remembered also as the time of the rebirth of Indio's Date Festival, begun in 1921. The event was repeated in 1922 with exhibits and excursions to date gardens. Not until 1941 was there another date industry celebration. In that year a fair was planned and held in its own giant tent and in September ground was broken for the first permanent buildings.

This outdoor stage, designed and constructed by Harry Oliver, was built at a cost of $25,000. His movie credits include sets for *Ben Hur, Viva Villa,* and *The Good Earth.* He was also well known for publishing the *Desert Rat Scrap Book,* and the construction of Old Fort Oliver in Thousand Palms, both in the 1940s. (Courtesy of Anita Carter Ellis)

The Arabian Nights Pageant has been presented nightly during the Date Festival, free to all visitors, for more than fifty years. (Courtesy of Anita Carter Ellis)

George Ames, manager of the 1941 show, recalled that the entire forty acres, where the present fair grounds and county buildings are, was available for $10,000, but it took considerable persuasion by the Indio Civic Club to get the county to make the purchase.

World War II came along and activities were suspended until 1947 when an Arabian theme was officially adopted. In May, Louise Dardenelle, artist and poet, and Harry Oliver, whose Hollywood background included Academy Awards for set designs, put their heads together and the idea of the Arabian Nights

Lead singer Anita Carter Ellis, Luke Christiansen, and another cast member pose before one of the walls carrying out the Arabic motif. (Courtesy of Anita Carter Ellis)

Cecelia Foulkes portrays one of the visitors to the Garden Tomb in the Mecca Easter Pagaent.

Pageant came into being. A script was created and a stage, recalling an Oriental marketplace and a Caliph's palace, was built. First performance was in 1948, using a script prepared by Louise Dardenelle, who died tragically in December 1947.

In the beginning, and for the next five years, the pageant was "hometown" from start to finish. Professional excellence was shown by the locals. Anita Carter Ellis and Wynne and Alex Hammond had leading roles in the 1948 production. The pageant was an overwhelming success and attracted the attention of *Life* magazine. Harry Oliver's dramatic outdoor stage was stunning, contributing greatly to the magic of the production. Anita Ellis was chosen to write the 1950 script. She evolved a story, which though an original one, contained the romance and suspense of an Arabian Nights Tale. Again, there was dancing, singing, gorgeous costumes, and vari-colored lights to complete the story laid in the city of Bagdad. Literally hundreds of local citizens have participated in the pageant over the fifty years of its presentation. Lead singers, in addition to those mentioned, include Gwen Harlow, Doug Caplette, Eve Bowlin, Cecelia Foulkes, Paul Villalobos, and Bill Wool, supported by a chorus of community singers, dancers, and costumemakers.

A Queen Scheherazade was selected in 1947, and since that date a Date Festival Queen and Princesses have been chosen from contestants representing Riverside County cities. Bob Fullenwider, the fair manager for many years, deserves much credit for overseeing the development of the permanent facilities and the ongoing

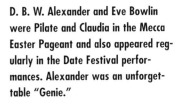

D. B. W. Alexander and Eve Bowlin were Pilate and Claudia in the Mecca Easter Pageant and also appeared regularly in the Date Festival performances. Alexander was an unforgettable "Genie."

Alex and Wynne Hammond were not only lead singers in the Date Festival performances, but also in the Mecca Easter Pageant.

Worshippers at the annual Sunrise Service at Travertine Point could imagine they were in Palestine, looking out over the Sea of Galilee. Cars lining Highway 99 attest to the popularity of this Easter morning event.

activities of the fair. Credit, too, should be given to Carmen Shelton, who, with the local Soroptimist club promoted the wearing of Arabian costumes by merchants and fairgoers, adding greatly to the "color" of the festival.

The Mecca Easter Pageant, "The Master Passes By" was presented in an outdoor amphitheater in Box Canyon in the late 1940s and early 1950s. Annual Easter Sunrise services were an interdenominational tradition, held at Travertine Point, overlooking the Salton Sea.

Airport Boulevard heads straight for the western mountains and the present location of PGA West, going past the greatly expanded Coachella Valley High School. It served students from Palm Desert to the Salton Sea and east to Desert Center.

Enjoying golf in Palm Desert was this trio made up of Randolph Scott, Dwight Eisenhower, and Freeman Gosden. (Courtesy of Palm Desert Historical Society)

Coachella Valley

New Cities

Chapter Ten

Palm Desert

Before there was a Palm Desert, this was the view looking west from the dune north of Grand Champions Resort (Courtesy of Palm Desert Historical Society)

In the early 1920s there were scattered farms on the sandy plain north of present Highway 111 in Palm Desert. Grapes, dates, and citrus were the favored crops, but it was a long way to the railroad, and roads were poor. Then, during World War II, General George Patton needed a place for his motor pool and he chose what was then known as "Palm Village." The headquarters was on what is now Portola Avenue. By the end of the war, Palm Village was a cluster of six houses and a few farms—one of which belonged to Edgar Bergen.

The Shadow Mountain Club was a real oasis with both swimming pool and lake. (Courtesy of Palm Desert Historical Society)

Typical of celebrities who enjoyed the club were Mr. and Mrs. Harold Lloyd. (Courtesy of Palm Desert Historical Society)

Wells were drilled with varying success, but a friend of Bergen, Cliff Henderson, and his brothers, recognized the rugged beauty of the area and they envisioned a romantic resort. The group sank a well 660 feet deep, discovered a substantial source of good water, and the Shadow Mountain Club development was underway. The club opened in 1946 with a beautiful clubhouse, its own man-made lake, and a large figure-eight swimming pool. Hollywood celebrity friends of the developers flocked there to enjoy the sunny climate and to participate in laying out a new town.

Randall Henderson built a Southwest-style building in 1948. His periodical, *The Desert Magazine*, was published there, and an impressive gallery of desert paintings was a feature of the building. Henderson's magazine created enough volume for a post office to be authorized in 1947. Bud Godfrey's Village Market opened in 1946, Ed Mullin's Pharmacy in 1951, and Bob Keedy's soda fountain in 1957.

The settlement north of Highway 111 was still known as Palm Village. In 1951 it merged with Palm Desert, south of the highway. By 1960 there were three thousand full-time residents. El Paseo Drive was envisioned by Cliff Henderson as a "nice place to shop," and in the late 1940s it was lined with signs suggesting the stores that might ultimately be built there. Golf courses came next, with the Shadow Mountain course opening in 1959, Palm Desert Country Club in 1962, and Marrakesh and Del Safari (now Avondale) in 1969. Ironwood's first course opened in 1973 and was washed away by a huge flood coming from Dead Indian

Canyon in 1976. Fairway condominium complexes became a popular housing choice for golf enthusiasts.

This aerial view of the new College of the Desert campus was taken December 5, 1963. The architect chose to echo the stately trunks of the campus date garden on the outside walls and in the columns supporting its covered walkways. (Courtesy of Palm Desert Historical Society)

Dr. Roy McCall, on left, was the first president of the College of the Desert. With him is Harry Cannon. (Courtesy of Palm Desert Historical Society)

Velma McCall was the gracious "First Hostess" on the new campus. (Courtesy of Palm Desert Historical Society)

College of the Desert, Coachella Valley's first college, was built in 1962, and its campus now provides space for classes offered by California State University San Bernardino. Bandleader Fred Waring dreamed of a theater in Palm Desert, and for years he gave concerts in the gymnasium of College of the Desert to raise funds for a suitable building. Fulfillment of the dream—the McCallum Theater—is an elegant venue for all manner of musical and theatrical performances.

The Living Desert, a 1,200-acre wildlife and botanical sanctuary, opened in 1970, part of Philip Boyd's original holdings. It interprets the desert to thousands of children and adults annually and is one of the prime attractions of the Coachella Valley.

Palm Desert voted to incorporate in 1973. Its central location made it an ideal spot for retail businesses to locate, and the completion of Ernest Hahn's Palm Desert Town Center in 1984 established the city as the shopping center of the valley. Desert Crossings and El Paseo Drive have added to Palm Desert's appeal to shoppers.

Desert Beautiful, dedicated to encouraging efforts to keep Coachella Valley clean and beautiful, has its roots in Palm Desert. Marian Henderson has for years headed this most worthwhile organization which benefits the entire valley. The dream she shared with her husband, Cliff Henderson, has become a reality.

Rancho Mirage

"Mail Box Row" created a sense of community in the 1930s. Neighbors lived acres apart and meeting at the mail box built friendships. One resident remembered sitting around bonfires in the winter, socializing and making plans for Rancho Mirage.

Travelers along the old Bradshaw Stage Route to the gold fields near La Paz, Arizona, passed through present-day Rancho Mirage. Most planned to stop at Palm Springs and Indian Wells, known watering spots. Interestingly, Rancho Mirage is almost halfway between the two towns. By 1915 there was a graded road instead of just wagon ruts, and farming had spread to the valley floor below Magnesia Falls Canyon. *Wonder Palms Date Ranch*, developed by the DaVall family, was one of the first in the area.

Los Angeles developers R. P. Davie and E. E. McIntyre recognized the potential of the spot. They purchased hundreds of acres from the Southern Pacific Railroad. William E. Everett homesteaded and built the *Eleven Mile Ranch*. Davie himself made a road through the deep gully cut by the Whitewater River in its 1916 flood. He named the road "Rio del Sol," and the *Desert Sun* newspaper likened the achievement to the opening of the Panama Canal!

In 1928 the Southland Land and Realty Company bought 160 acres of Everett's land with the notion of re-creating the entire Nile valley, complete with tents, camels, and pyramids. The stock market crash of 1929 changed those plans, but news of the area's charm spread through the Hollywood community and stars like Frank Morgan bought homes in the cove.

In 1934 Dr. Earl Tarr, a Los Angeles pediatrician, opened a school for asthmatic children on *Eleven Mile Ranch*. Will Rogers' death in a plane crash ended his promised funding, but a group of Rogers' friends, including Basil Rathbone, Mary Pickford, and Tom Mix, helped underwrite expenses of the school which operated until World War II.

There are several theories as to the naming of Rancho Mirage. One of them credits Mrs. Louis Blankenhorn with commenting on the misty green of the area along Rio Del Sol, when viewed from the upper cove, saying it resembled a "mirage." The word "rancho" was added for sales appeal. In 1934 the Rancho Mirage Community Association was officially recorded in Sacramento.

Development slowed during the war years, but took off again after the war. Hank Gogerty opened the Desert Air Hotel—with airport and a polo field adjacent to the runway. *White Sun Guest Ranch*, established by Jack Dengler in 1946, was the successor to the old *Eleven Mile Ranch*.

Thunderbird Dude Ranch, managed by Frank Bogert, became Thunderbird Country Club, with the desert's first eighteen-hole golf course. Hollywood couples like Phil Harris and Alice Faye, and corporate executives became its first residents, and parties at the club were legendary. Other country clubs followed, giving Rancho Mirage reason to call itself the "Country Club City."

Rancho Mirage has hosted every United States President since President Truman, and one former President, Gerald Ford, has made it his retirement home. Another of its most distinguished residents, Ambassador Walter Annenberg, built his estate, *Sunnylands*, at the corner of Wonder Palms Road and Rio Del Sol, now known as Frank Sinatra and Bob Hope Drives. Since 1961,

Johnny and Ruth Warburton load onions on their ranch in 1946, at the present site of Thunderbird Country Club. The Warburtons were under contract to MGM Studios.

In 1946 Hank Gogerty opened the Desert Air Hotel, the desert's first fly-in hotel and airport on what is currently the site of Rancho Las Palmas Resort and Country Club on Bob Hope Drive. (Courtesy of Palm Desert Historical Society)

world leaders have been guests in his 32,000-square-foot main house and guest quarters.

This aerial view of Rancho Mirage shows how essential it is to have the channels that carry stormwater safely from the canyon and into the Whitewater River. At one time the river was a barrier to development out into the valley plain. The present controlled channel is clearly visible across the center of the picture. (Courtesy of Coachella Valley Water District)

Commercial development followed, primarily along the Highway 111 corridor. In 1966 Bob Hope donated eighty acres on Rio Del Sol for a proposed five-million-dollar medical center. Completed in 1971 and named for Dwight Eisenhower, it was dedicated by then President Richard Nixon, Mamie Eisenhower, and then Governor Ronald Reagan.

In this 1964 photograph, Otho Moore points out the Whitewater River bank north of Rancho Mirage, cut away in the 1916 flood.

Concerned citizens met to plan incorporation, spurred on by efforts of Palm Desert and Cathedral City to extend their influence into the Rancho Mirage area. An election was held and on August 3, 1973, Rancho Mirage was officially declared the sixteenth city in Riverside County. Recognizing the celebrities who have called Rancho Mirage home, the city has named streets for Bob Hope, Gerald Ford, Ginger Rogers, Dinah Shore, and Frank Sinatra.

From 1927 to 1946 these handsome stone pillars held a sign which spanned Highway 111, welcoming visitors to the city. (Courtesy of Bob and Kay Hillery)

Cathedral City

From 1927 to 1946 these handsome stone pillars held a sign which spanned Highway 111, welcoming visitors to the city. (Courtesy of Bob and Kay Hillery)

An 1850s survey party, under the command of Colonel Henry Washington, is credited with naming Cathedral Canyon. They were impressed with the "cathedral-like" look of the deep canyon and gave it a name, since none appeared on their maps. When the original subdivision maps were filed in 1925, the developers of the alluvial fan which spread out at the mouth of the canyon named the site Cathedral City.

Cathedral City had four founders. They set about acquiring tracts of land from the Southern Pacific Railroad, and selling lots to the people who were flocking to the desert. On the opening day of sales, in January 1926, a large crowd attended a barbeque and listened to a sales pitch. Historical records indicate many lots were sold. The four men who combined their talents to develop a new city were George Allen and Jack Grove, who were real estate men; Glenn Plumley, who had worked for the Southern Pacific;

In 1925 George and Luella Allen built the first house in town at the southeast corner of Cathedral Canyon Drive and Highway 111. (Courtesy of Bob and Kay Hillery)

and M. V. Van Fleet, who had just sold his linoleum business to Armstrong. Van Fleet furnished much-needed development capital.

In the 1930s the newly paved highway brought added business. (Courtesy of Bob and Kay Hillery and Fraser Photos)

Cathedral City's first post office also functioned as the general store, gas station, and home of the first postmistress, Edna Cobb. In 1927, the State Highway was paved, and increased traffic justified the building of several motels and a restaurant. There were two gaming casinos which closed at the start of World War II. The first one-room school opened in 1941 with twenty-four students in grades one to six.

Incorporated in 1981, the city has grown steadily both in population and in geographical area, stretching from its original cove location across the desert to Interstate 10.

In 1941, Bob Hillery proudly displays the flag at opening-day ceremonies for the first school. Hillery is George Allen's nephew, and his collection of pictures and realia chronicle the city's history. He credits the Chamber of Commerce, established in 1937, with being the driving force behind all civic improvements. (Courtesy of Bob and Kay Hillery)

A 1960 view of Cathedral City, with Date Palm Drive in the foreground. (Courtesy of Bob and Kay Hillery)

Desert Hot Springs

Located atop the San Andreas fault, Desert Hot Springs has long attracted people to its natural warm springs. Cahuilla Indians were the first to enjoy its waters. Before 1900, government survey parties spotted a warm spring and noted on their maps "Two bunches of palms." The name of that place was shortened to "Two Bunch Palms"—a name that is used by the resort at that location today.

The first white settler was Cabot Yerxa, a descendant of the Cabots of Boston. He came in 1913, walking into the desert from Banning. He set to work to "prove up" a 160-acre homestead. Reopening an old Indian well, he found hot mineral water. He dug another well and found cold water, leading him to name his place *Miracle Hill*. After a series of absences, he came back to work on his masterpiece, a Hopi Indian-style pueblo. Built by hand, without blueprints, Yerxa worked on it from 1944 almost until his death in 1965. It has 35 rooms, 65 doors, and 150 windows and has been designated a State Point of Historical Interest.

I. W. Coffee gave Desert Hot Springs its name and became its first developer in the 1930s, but growth was very slow during the Depression. Lots were offered at $200 to $400 each, with few takers. The famous and infamous came—Hollywood stars and supposedly Al Capone. It was rumored that Capone built a hideaway at Two Bunch Palms. Commercial bath houses and hotels sprang up. By 1945 there were three hundred homes and one hundred commercial structures. By 1963 there were more than two hundred mineral therapeutic pools.

Desert Hot Springs was incorporated September 17, 1963, unique among valley cities since it had neither an agricultural nor a railroad beginning.

Cabot Yerxa's pueblo stands as his tribute to Indian people. (Courtesy of Palm Springs Historical Society)

Part IV–Valley-wide Concerns

George Ames and Shaler Wilder demonstrate just how hot the street can get as they fry an egg on the pavement in Indio.

Keeping Cool

Summers in the Coachella Valley were a real challenge in the days before air-conditioning, fancy swimming pools, or even electric fans. Then, as now, many just left during the hottest months, perhaps to a cabin near Idyllwild, or to the beach. But people found ingenious ways of "beating the heat." This photograph essay details some of the solutions:

A tent house could be completely shaded by a roof made of the fronds of the native fan palms.

Tennis was popular at the turn of the century, played on the court behind the railroad depot. The roadmaster's home features the double roof which shaded the building.

A family tries to rest on a hot summer afternoon in 1904, upstairs on the porch of the Southern Pacific Hotel in Indio. Wrapping up in a wet sheet was another solution.

Coachella Valley

This one-room dwelling was named a "submarine," not because it was built below sea level but because the sleeper was under water! Water was piped to the roof and allowed to drip over the top and flow down the sides, reducing the temperature by 15 to 20 degrees.

Swimming parties at the ranches were very popular. Generally the reservoir served as storage for the run-off of artesian wells and it doubled as a swimming pool. (Coachella Valley Water District photograph)

The watering tank at the U.S. Date Garden in Indio provided a great swimming pool for Stewart Nixon, Margaret Moore, and Jean Barger in the summer of 1937.

Coachella Valley

Ryerson Stumak Thackery Crawford ~~Lunch~~ Nixon Bargier Moore

Just to prove that it wasn't always HOT, this November 1937 photograph shows three of the fathers of the children in the watering tank, and personnel from the Riverside Citrus Station, dressed for winter.

In 1949 Hotel Indio guests enjoyed the sun in its front garden, while being able to retreat to a comfortable room cooled by the new evaporative coolers.

The Salton Sea attracted swimmers, water skiers, and particularly speedboat enthusiasts. Gold Cup races attracted some of the fastest boats in the world. The official program in 1948 noted, "The boats are up to 40 feet in length, weigh up to 2 1/2 tons and are powered by motors developing as high as 1500 horsepower. It is not uncommon for boats of this class to clear the water for distances of sixty to eighty feet."

"Low barometric pressure and greater water density make the Salton Sea the fastest body of water in the world for speedboat racing," proclaimed an article in *National Motorist* for January-February 1950. That's twenty years after a Salton Sea Race Program made the front page of the *Coachella Submarine* newspaper of December 13, 1929. Much of the credit for these races goes to a small group of local racing enthusiasts. At the 1951 Regatta, twenty-one World Records were set.

In 1948, a crowd gathered to watch the launching of *Hurricane IV*, owned by Morlan Visel. The boat had broken many Gold Cup records.

Kay Olesen and Glenn Gurley of Indio flank the trophy awarded to the Gold Cup winner. Boat owners included Henry J. Kaiser, Horace Dodge, and local driver, Dr. Louis Novotny.

Coachella Valley

Of course, there were pretty girls to enjoy the excitement of the races.

There was excitement and community support for the Salton Sea Regattas.

New World's Speed Records for airplanes were also set over the Salton Sea. *North American Aviation* released this picture and news story. A North American F-100 Super Sabre hit 767 miles per hour on one pass and averaged 754.98 over a 15-kilometer course. The "sizzling" dash was made by Air Force Lieutenant Colonel F. K. (Pete) Everest. "Keeping cool" were the photographers at the sea's edge.

Running out of gas was a hazard of driving in the desert—with few service stations outside of town. (Paul Ames photograph)

Roads and Travel

"Road" was a term that defied description in the early days of the valley. Tracks through the sand connected homes and towns before 1910. Ranchers kept the ruts of roads well packed with straw to keep cars and wagons from becoming stuck. There was considerable consternation one hot afternoon when someone on the Sandy Corner road, near Thermal, accidentally dropped a lighted "roll-your-own" on the road and the road literally burned up!

North-south travel between towns was best accomplished on the train. A horse and wagon or buggy was one's best bet for east-west travel. The road out of the valley from Indio was a sandy trail which left the town-site border and wound its way northwest past Point Happy, through a mesquite tunnel in Indian Wells, then on to the village of Palm Springs and up the grade to Whitewater, Cabazon, Banning and Beaumont. Much credit must be given to the early citizens who found the will and the money to establish a road system on the valley floor.

The Coachella Valley Road Committee, headed by J. W. Wilson, worked for many years to secure support for a road to connect the valley with the cool country in the San Jacinto mountains. In 1930, the county supervisors authorized the construction of a gravel road. Completed in 1932, it was paved in the late 1930s, becoming the present Highway 74. The old road up from Banning was long and steep. Sometimes cars had to back up hills so that gravity would keep the gasoline flowing from the under-the-front-seat gas tank to the carburetor.

This is thought to be the site of one of the old Bradshaw Stage stops near Thousand Palms. The Bradshaw Trail was the valley's first "road."

This was the main road to the Colorado River, Dale Mining District, and Cottonwood Springs in the 1920s.

E. N. T. Burnett, owner of the Ford Agency in Coachella, captioned this 1922 photograph, "Should have known better."

This photograph, published in *The Date Palm* in 1914 shows the grading equipment used in roadbuilding in the westside area now occupied by PGA West.

Securing a paved highway from Edom to Indio was a justly celebrated event. The sign on the right states, "WARNING. ADVISARY TO GO BY PALM SPRINGS DURING WIND STORM." (Tom Mullan photograph)

Opening of the Palms to Pines road was recognized by this group which includes Win and Josephine Wilson, Art Wood, and Doctor June McCarroll.

This is a 1944 view of the Desert Tavern, on Highway 99 in Coachella, which served the motoring public and locals.

The Desert Tavern made a good rest stop for tourists traveling to and from the Imperial Valley.

Clark's Historic 99 Truck Stop and Store is the successor to Abernathy's Truck Stop, built in 1948, when Highway 99 was the celebrated artery from Mexico to the Canadian border. It passed through the center of Indio.

Locals enjoy a Box Canyon picnic, circa 1920.

The Southern Pacific built this infirmary, which had two beds and a nurse on duty, about 1897.

Health Care

About 1903, N. O. Nelson opened an Indio Health Camp which was west of the depot and about one hundred feet north of the tracks. People came seeking improvement and healing of respiratory ailments.

Before 1900, the Southern Pacific Railroad built and staffed a small infirmary in Indio, primarily to care for railroad employees, and trains provided transportation for the seriously ill or injured to doctors and hospitals in the cities to the west. Several doctors set up sanitariums in Palm Springs to care for those who came seeking relief from tuberculosis and other respiratory ailments, but it was not until Dr. June Robertson arrived in 1904 that the valley had a resident family physician.

Dr. June Robertson came in 1904 because of her husband's tubercular condition. She intended to be "just a housewife" but need propelled her into the job of caring for the sick of Coachella Valley. (Courtesy of Coachella Valley Water District)

"Doc June" covered the valley from Palm Springs to the Salton Sea. She took over supervision of the health camp until it closed in 1908, served the railroad and farm families, and, in 1907, was appointed by the Bureau of Indian Affairs to be doctor to the valley Indian reservations.

"Doc June's" territory ranged from Palm Springs to the Salton Sea. There were no real roads to the scattered ranches so she soon abandoned her buggy for a saddle on a spirited horse. Sickness and births came at all hours. A three-hour ride, across rain-swollen washes to deliver a baby in the middle of the night, was not uncommon. On one occasion she took a railroad handcar from Edom to the home of one of the section hands, arriving ten minutes ahead of the stork. Many an operation was performed on the kitchen table, under the glow of a kerosene lamp. She said, "I always carried my instruments with me for it was a long, dusty ride back to the office and there were no telephones. I didn't do major surgery, but I took out lots of tonsils."

In 1914 Mr. Robertson died and two years later "Doc June" married Frank McCarroll, the station agent at Indio. In that same year, other doctors set up offices in the valley and she retired to participate in civic affairs, and, most notably, to successfully promote the idea of a centerline down the newly paved highways of the state.

The influenza epidemic of 1918 kept Dr. S. S. M. Jennings busy. He ordered schools closed and advised that children sleep outside in the fresh air if their parents were ill. There was no effective treatment for influenza, which did not itself kill, but the complicating pneumonia, in the days before antibiotics, killed one out of every two patients.

Dr. S. S. M. Jennings came in 1916, primarily to farm, but seeing the need, he, too, became doctor to the whole community. As school district doctor, he led the fight against "pink eye," a real valley scourge until the Coachella Valley Mosquito Abatement District's eye-gnat eradication program reduced the problem. (Courtesy of Coachella Valley Water District)

Dr. Harry Smiley set up practice in Indio in 1921. He and his bride were on their way from Arkansas to Los Angeles to begin a medical career there, but their car broke down in Box Canyon. Unable to afford repairs, and discovering that Indio had no doctor, they decided to stay in the valley. Their adobe home in Indio now houses the Coachella Valley Historical Society and Museum.

Charlie Green inspects the Box Canyon road which proved too much for the Smiley car. All east-west traffic went through Box Canyon.

Coachella Valley

In 1928, Dr. Russell Gray built Indio's first real hospital at the corner of Miles and Towne Avenues.

Health Care

Drs. Smiley and Gray came in the early 1920s. Dr. Gray's hospital, opened in 1928, qualified as an A1-rated facility after just one year of operation. It consisted of three bungalows moved onto one lot in downtown Indio. With the assistance of his wife, who was a trained nurse, they managed to care for, and even make house calls to the six thousand patients in the area.

During the building of the Metropolitan Aqueduct, Dr. Sidney Garfield built Contractor's General Hospital near Desert Center. Garfield is remembered as the originator of prepaid medical insurance. He found it difficult to collect for medical service from men who were making $4 to $5 per day, and the companies that provided industrial accident coverage to the contractors were reluctant to direct patients to Garfield's small hospital. He was going broke when he presented the idea of a nickel-a-day payroll deduction plan to the contractors. They liked the idea and over 90 percent of the men signed up for unlimited medical care from Garfield.

Garfield's desert practice flourished. When the aqueduct job was finished, Garfield moved to Grand Coulee Dam in Washington State and during World War II he set up prepaid health plans at major shipyards. After the war, with the backing of Henry J. Kaiser, he founded Kaiser Permanente, a preeminent healthcare provider today.

Dr. B. Gene Morris worked with Dr. Garfield at the small hospital which cared for aqueduct workers in the 1930s. When he returned to Indio, he built Casita Hospital, near the western edge of the city. With Coachella Valley Hospital, it served the area until it was joined by Desert Hospital in Palm Springs in the winter of 1951.

Dr. Reynaldo Carreon provided eye care
to hundreds of desert residents.
(Courtesy of Carreon Foundation)

Meanwhile, in 1935 Dr. Clair Johnson built and operated
Valley Maternity Hospital in Mecca, and Dr. B. Gene Morris built
Casita Hospital in Indio. It later became Valley Memorial
Hospital, then merged with Indio Community Hospital, built on
Monroe Street, on land originally owned by Dr. Reynaldo
Carreon, a noted Los Angeles opthamologist. Carreon maintained
a home and office in Indio and provided eye care to hundreds of
desert residents. Carreon had a passion for helping Hispanic young
people receive the higher education responsible for his own success
in life, and his scholarships enabled many to go on to school.

Indio Community Hospital became John F. Kennedy Memorial Hospital in 1984. (Courtesy of JFK Hospital)

Coachella Valley

Eunice Kennedy Shriver spoke at the John F. Kennedy Memorial Hospital dedication. (Courtesy of JFK Hospital)

Desert Hospital in Palm Springs; Eisenhower Hospital in Rancho Mirage; and John F. Kennedy Memorial Hospital, successor to Indio Community Hospital, now provide valley residents with the best medical care available. Coachella Valley has come a long way from the tireless work of a woman doctor on horseback, who operated on a kitchen table and put her most serious cases on the next westbound Southern Pacific train.

Controlling Floods

For thousands of years, the Whitewater River and the streams that flowed periodically out of the canyons surrounding the valley had run harmlessly into the desert sands. They replenished the valley's great underground aquifer. Early writers spoke of the mouth of the Whitewater River "at Windy Point, west of Palm Springs." From there water just fanned out into countless sandy washes. The drainage area of this river encompasses a watershed of 2,038 miles. Adding to the problem of control is the fact that narrowing the channel would necessarily increase the depth. The Whitewater River course, from Palm Springs to the Salton Sea, maintains a fall that is greater in its 50-mile length than that of the Mississippi River from above St. Louis, Missouri, to the Gulf of Mexico. The fall of the riverbed is 90 feet per mile at Windy Point.

The flood of January 1916 separated the railroad depot from the Gard store and the rest of the town.

After the 1916 flood, probably the worst of modern times, there was a somewhat defined channel clear to Point Happy. After that, the water spread across the desert, most of it disappearing before it reached the Salton Sink. Debris from floodwaters built layers of gravel, sand, silt, and clay. On the west side of the valley, well drillers found boulders as deep as 200 feet below the surface, demonstrating the violence of ancient floods. Today, golf courses, subdivisions, towns and ranches sit astride these natural flood courses. The present stormwater drain from Point Happy to the Salton Sea has been aligned, constructed, and maintained by local people to make use of the valley floor possible.

Prior to 1915, people with investments in ranches and new developments around Indio, Coachella, and Thermal, realized that a concerted effort had to be made to tame the flows. Two small districts had been operating—the Indio Levee District and the Coachella Stormwater District. In 1915, in a valleywide election, the Coachella Valley Stormwater District was organized, and its three directors agreed to complete as soon as possible the storm drain started by the Indio Levee District. A four-mile levee was proposed, and one mile of that levee had been completed at the upper end when the flood of January 1916 hit. Interestingly, the width of Oasis Street in Indio is so because it was to be the site of a levee, for which rights-of-way had been obtained.

In 1927 floodwaters out of Deep Canyon washed out several miles of roadways before reaching the Whitewater River channel. This scene is at the southwest corner of Cook Street and Highway 111. Property owners in the area, with the Stormwater District's assistance, built the present channel along the foothills in Indian Wells to divert later floods and avert continuing damage. (Courtesy of Coachella Valley Water District)

Coachella Valley

The winter snow pack was heavy, the weather warmed, and more than four inches of rain fell at Beaumont and Cabazon in two weeks. The storm moved from west to east. Floodwaters washed out eleven miles of Southern Pacific roadbed between Whitewater and Thousand Palms. Indio was under a mile-wide sheet of water, with water two feet deep on Fargo Street. Coachella, Thermal, and Mecca were under water and many miles of county roads were damaged. Nine passenger trains were marooned in Indio for more than five days, taxing food supplies. The Whitewater River's meandering channel had become narrowed and scoured up to fifty feet deep between Cathedral City and Point Happy, creating a new mouth of the river at Point Happy. Supplies were brought up from Yuma, carried by men walking the ties that sagged over the washed out areas south of Indio.

Northwest of Indio, the 1927 flood damaged the railroad trestle, the highway bridge, and telegraph and telephone lines.

Warm rains melted the snowpack in February 1927, causing another severe flood. Thousand Palms Wash runoff undermined the bridge at Myoma, and Deep Canyon floodwaters washed out 1,500 feet of highway at *Cook's Ranch* in Palm Desert, cutting a channel nearly 10 feet deep.

Coachella was awash in the 1939 flood.

Successive heavy rains continued to plague the valley. There was no effective control of floodwaters until the completion of the protective dikes on the east side of the valley, and various dikes and stormwater channels at the mouth of canyons on the west side of the valley. Credit should be given to those farsighted early residents, who, through the storm water district and the county water district, began to take measures early both to conserve floodwaters and add them to the underground basin, and to plan for the future protection of the rapidly developing valley. There has been a continual upgrade and realignment of facilities as needs dictate, including the construction of a new "Lake Cahuilla" as a terminal reservoir for the All-American Canal. Besides providing regulatory storage for irrigation water, it can also impound floodwaters.

Water poured down Box Canyon, east of Mecca, at the height of the stick held by J. Win Wilson, editor of *The Date Palm* newspaper. Floods did severe damage to property on the east side of the valley and in 1941 contributed to the push to build the present East Side Dike. It protects the Coachella Canal and the eastern portion of the valley.

The 1939 flood accounted for this picture of Mecca under water.

Today's Lake Cahuilla is the terminus of the All-American Canal and a popular recreation spot. (Courtesy of Coachella Valley Water District)

Enough Water—The Essential for Growth

"Conceived in adversity, created to meet a desperate need, nourished on the faith and determination of pioneers, the Coachella Valley Water District's story is a saga of reclamation magic," wrote valley historian, Ole Nordland.

The story begins as early as 1917. Seven thousand acres of brush had been cleared from Indian Wells to the Salton Sea. The water level in wells was going down. Land development was slowing. Adding to the urgency of the situation was a plan proposed at an El Centro meeting to build a canal from Palm Springs to the Imperial Valley. It would carry water from the Whitewater River, Arrastre Creek, Pipes Creek, and Snow Creek for domestic use in the towns of the Imperial Valley. A portion would be left for irrigation purposes in the Coachella Valley.

Citizens held mass meetings in Thermal and Coachella and petitions to form a Coachella Valley County Water District were circulated. An all-valley election was held in January 1918 at which 324 citizens voted for the creation of the district; 49 were opposed. Polling places were designated at Coachella, Thermal, Indian Wells, Mecca, Edom, Indio, and Palm Springs. Cabazon voters came to the Palm Springs railroad station to cast their ballots. How much we owe to those 324 voters! The district's stated purpose was (1) to protect the underground waters by filing on the streams entering the Whitewater River Basin, (2) to conserve the water entering the basin, and (3) to seek a supplemental water supply.

The Coachella Canal hugs the eastern foothills, then turns west above Indio, bringing the water which literally makes today's valley growth possible. (Courtesy of Coachella Valley Water District)

"Swing with Swing" was the 1925 slogan used to encourage votes for Senator Swing, coauthor of the bill that authorized the construction of Boulder Dam and the All-American Canal.

People had become aware of the efforts of the Imperial Irrigation District to obtain a new canal to replace the old Alamo Canal. It tapped the Colorado River at a point just below Yuma and carried it through Mexico to a location near Calexico. The new proposal would build an "All-American Canal" which would bring the water west on a route north of the international border. Its elevation would be high enough so that it could irrigate the East Mesa and north end of the Imperial Valley by gravity flow. The natural question was, "Why not extend an eastern highline canal branch to serve the Coachella Valley?"

Dr. S. S. M. Jennings was seated as president of the Board of Trustees of the newly formed district at its first meeting in May 1918. They immediately went to work implementing all three of their objectives. An engineer was hired at $150 per month to survey all of the wells from Point Happy to Palm Springs and to evaluate the possibilities of spreading storm waters over the area of sand dunes and gravel beds above Edom as a means of conserving water at a very small cost. Next came a long series of actions spanning thirty years which led to building the Coachella Branch of the All-American Canal and the delivery of the first water through the Coachella distribution system in March 1948. The new board began a relentless struggle for recognition of its need for Colorado River water and for the protection of its underground waters.

From its source in the mountains of Colorado, Wyoming, and Utah, water for the irrigation of farms in the Coachella Valley travels a total of 1,300 miles through the Grand Canyon and past a series of major dams, all of which played a part in the negotiations and litigation which ultimately secured a share of Colorado River water for California. There were major disagreements between advocates of building the dams for power production versus flood control and irrigation. The Boulder Dam project was linked in Congress with the All-American Canal Bill. The Swing-Johnson Bill was approved December 21, 1928, and signed by President Hoover, approving, among other things, the construction of the dam and the canal at a cost of about $165,000,000. Driving two Model-T Fords with wide-belted rims replacing the tires on the wheels, district trustees and Attorney Yager made a trip over the proposed route of the All-American Canal in April 1930.

Lowell Weeks, seated at left, with support staff Ole Nordland, Maurice Sherrill, and Walter Wright, deserves much credit for managing the district from 1956 until his retirement in 1986. (Courtesy of Coachella Valley Water District)

The Coachella Valley County Water District board spent years negotiating for its own allotment of Colorado River water. Had they become a part of the Imperial Irrigation District they would have had to assume a share of its large indebtedness. Finally a separate contract was drawn for construction of the Coachella Branch of the All-American Canal and for Coachella Valley's share of other costs. The names of the water district's heroes are many, but the list would surely include such courageous men as Dr. S. S. Jennings, Thomas C. Yager, R. W. Blackburn, Chester Sparey, Dr. Harry Forbes, Truman Gridley, Lee Anderson, J. W. Newman, Ted Buck, Keith Farrar, Leon Kennedy, and Ray Rummonds. They fought the battles in Congress, in Sacramento, and in the Coachella and Imperial Valleys.

The Coachella Valley's underground water system is recognized worldwide as an outstanding example of efficiency and water conservation. The telemetering system is state-of-the-art. Through five hundred miles of pipeline, water is delivered to the valley's ranches. (Courtesy of Coachella Valley Water District)

The first 43.4 miles of the canal were completed in June 1940 and the second section was under construction. The board decided to deliver water to each 40-acre parcel and to use an underground pipe delivery system. World War II intervened and it was not until 1948 that the canal and its distribution system were completed. Local farmers listed five thousand acres available for growing guayule (for making synthetic rubber) in an effort to move the canal project up the priority list for funding. In February 1949, the U.S. Bureau of Reclamation agreed to a proposal to turn over to the board the operation of the Coachella Branch from the lowest turnout for the East Mesa to the end of the canal at Avenue 57. Completion of the flood control dikes, Lake Cahuilla, and all of the laterals has gone on to the present. Coachella Valley Water District headquarters in Coachella hosts engineers and tourists from all over the world who come to view the system and study its efficiency.

A water district *zanjero* turns on the water for a west side ranch. (Courtesy of Coachella Valley Water District)

This photograph shows the Coachella Valley Water District Headquarters in Coachella. The district began domestic water service in 1961. (Courtesy of Coachella Valley Water District)

Young date trees stand alongside mature date gardens, insuring the continuation of the valley's trademark crop. (Photograph courtesy of Oasis Date Gardens)

The ancient beach line at the base of our western mountains is quite visible from the 15th hole of the Arnold Palmer Private Course at PGA West in La Quinta. (Photograph courtesy of PGA West)

The Valley Today

Part 5–The Valley Today

By careful planning and resource management, farms, golf courses, and nine incorporated cities coexist today in the Coachella Valley. The cities, and their dates of incorporation are: Indio (1930), Palm Springs (1938), Coachella (1946), Desert Hot Springs (1963), Indian Wells (1967), Rancho Mirage (August 1973), Palm Desert (November 1973), Cathedral City (1981), and La Quinta (1982). In addition, there are the unincorporated communities of Thousand Palms, Bermuda Dunes, Thermal, and Mecca. Coachella Valley has more than ninety golf courses, more per capita than any other part of the country, and the valley hosts some of the most prestigious golf tournaments, including the Bob Hope Classic. The agricultural industry is worth more than $300 million.

Not only has air-conditioning made year-round living comfortable, but the Palm Springs Aerial Tramway wisks passengers to the 8,516-foot level of Mt. San Jacinto, where temperatures are always at least twenty degrees cooler. Paved bicycle paths and broad palm-lined streets have replaced the sandy ruts of earlier days. Tennis was one of the few sports available to the valley's early residents, and it is enjoyed today on courts that have welcomed the world's top players. There are elegant and diverse shopping areas, theaters, and museums. Conventions are booked years in advance in the outstanding hotels and convention centers. The valley's first four-year college will be built at the corner of Cook Street and Frank Sinatra Drive under the auspices of California State University, San Bernardino, on land made available by the city of Palm Desert. Most recently, casinos and related businesses have brought new prosperity to local Indian tribes and have provided an additional job base for the area.

In 1998 there are still rugged mountainsides and natural desert floor to remind us of "the way it was." The Living Desert in Palm Desert presents and interprets desert ecology, and the setting aside of the 12,000-acre Nature Conservancy in Thousand Palms Canyon is the kind of good planning which will preserve the best of our natural beauty and will guarantee a bright future for this unique area.

Coachella Valley

The picturesque 5th hole of the Jack Nicklaus Private Course at PGA West in La Quinta. PGA West is a private residential country club community. There are five championship golf courses, clay and grass tennis courts, a fitness center, clubhouse, beautiful homes, lakes, and swimming pools which would astound the valley's early residents. This was once considered "The Westside," reached by a sandy track due west from Thermal. (Photograph courtesy of PGA West)

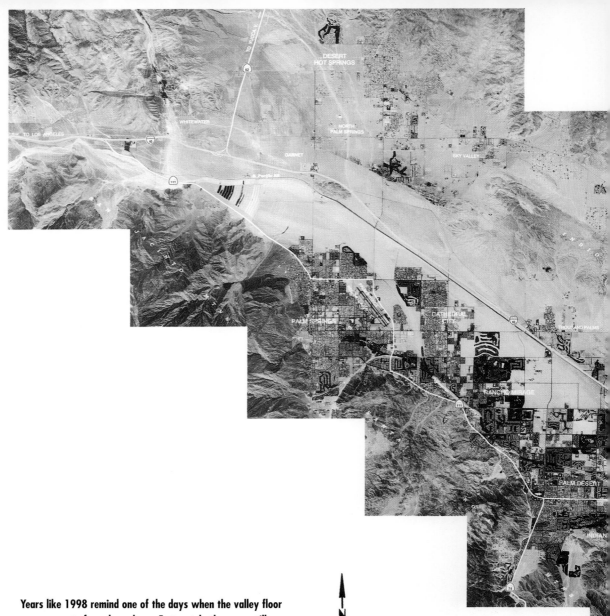

Years like 1998 remind one of the days when the valley floor was a carpet of purple verbena. Fortunately there are still areas where wildflowers bloom in profusion.

AERIAL FOTOBANK, INC — *DESERT MAP & AERIAL PHOTO*

© AERIAL FOTOBANK, INC.

COACHELLA VALLEY

This bobcat is one of local animals exhibited in nearly natural surroundings at The Living Desert, a twelve-hundred-acre wildlife and botanical park which preserves, protects, and interprets world deserts for delighted visitors. Sculptures of a cheetah family grace the entrance. (Photographs courtesy of The Living Desert)

Coachella Valley

View across a fairways at Del Webb's Sun City Palm Desert, looking west to the San Jacinto mountains. Sun City is a planned community of five thousand homes, built near the site of Apostle Palms Oasis, from which the Southern Pacific hauled water when they were building the railroad, and their station and yards at Indio in 1876. (Photograph courtesy of Sun City Palm Desert)

Polo and related equestrian events are a major attraction today. An estimated sixteen hundred horses take part annually in the Grand Prix at the Empire Equestrian Park. There are five polo fields, an International Horse Show complex, three arenas, an amphitheater, and a ten-acre grass event field. Many prestigious events are held here and at nearby Eldorado Polo Club. During the season, there are probably more horses in the valley today than there were in pioneer days. (Photograph courtesy of Empire Polo Club)

One of the most popular local events is the Empire Balloon, Wine and Polo Festival, combining popular balloon rides (available most of the year) and world-class polo matches.

Today's pools, like this one at Sun City Palm Desert, are a far cry from the farm reservoirs which were the swimming pools of Coachella Valley's pioneer families. (Photograph courtesy of Sun City Palm Desert)

Coachella Valley

Today's retirees look for, and find, active retirement living in the Coachella Valley.
(Photograph courtesy of Sun City Palm Desert)

The La Quinta Hotel is noted for its beautiful flower gardens, secluded cottages and unique setting at the base of the mountain spur originally named "Point Happy." (Photograph courtesy of The La Quinta Hotel)

Index

The La Quinta Hotel. (Photograph courtesy of The La Quinta Hotel)

About the Author

Patricia Laflin has lived in the Coachella Valley since 1950. Her husband, Ben, is the son of pioneer residents Ben and Lucy Laflin. Ben Sr. came to the valley in 1911 and became one of the valley's original date growers. Lucy came as a young teacher in 1916, married Ben, and stayed to instruct the valley's children for a third of a century.

Besides personally experiencing much of the valley's growth and changing face, Patricia was privileged to learn from the Laflins and their friends what it was like during the first half of the twentieth century when the groundwork was being laid for today's cities and its two major industries, agriculture and tourism. She worked with her family to develop Laflin Date Gardens and was named "Farmer of the Year" in 1987.

Patricia was a teacher and administrator in Thermal Union School District and Coachella Valley Unified School District for a total of twenty-one years. Her lifelong interest in history began as she grew up in Redding, California, surrounded by the gold mining country of Northern California. She won several history prizes for research and writing while still in high school and went on to study history and historical methods at the University of California, Berkeley, graduating with a bachelor's degree in history and a minor in English. She holds a master's degree in social science from Azuza Pacific University.

Patricia has written the *Periscope*, the annual publication of the Coachella Valley Historical Society for 1994, 1995, 1996, and 1997. Topics were "Living with Fires," "The Salton Sea," "Water for Millions," and "Coachella Valley Pioneer Women."

Besides writing for the historical society, Patricia has written numerous articles about the date industry, and publicity and sales materials for the family business. The five Laflin children grew up in Thermal, aware of the small town's promising beginning, and interested in the history their grandparents helped make.

Patricia and Ben now live in Bermuda Dunes, one of the valley's many golf-course communities—still interested in the date industry and in their twelve grandchildren.